LOVING
GOD
UP CLOSE

LOVING
GOD
UP CLOSE

REKINDLING

YOUR RELATIONSHIP

WITH THE HOLY SPIRIT

Calvin Miller

WARNER
Faith

A Division of AOL Time Warner Book Group

Scriptures noted NKJV are taken from the NEW KING JAMES VERSION. Copyright © 1979, 1980, 1982, Thomas Nelson, Inc., Publishers.

Scriptures noted NIV are taken from the HOLY BIBLE: NEW INTERNATIONAL VERSION®. Copyright © 1973, 1978, 1984 by International Bible Society. Used by permission of Zondervan Publishing House. All rights reserved.

Scriptures noted KJV are taken from the King James Version of the Bible.

Scriptures noted NASB are taken from the New American Standard Bible®, Copyright © 1960, 1962, 1963, 1968, 1972, 1975, 1977, 1995 by The Lockman Foundation. Used by permission.

Scriptures noted The Message are taken from *The Message: The New Testament in Contemporary English*. Copyright © 1993 by Eugene H. Peterson.

W WARNER *Faith* A Division of AOL Time Warner Book Group

Printed in the United States of America

First Warner Books printing: February 2004

10 9 8 7 6 5 4 3 2 1

Library of Congress Cataloging-in-Publication Data

Miller, Calvin.
    Loving God up close : rekindling your relationship with the Holy Spirit / Calvin Miller.
       p. cm.
Includes bibliographical references.
     ISBN 0-446-53012-3
   1. Holy Spirit. I. Title.
    BT121.3.M55 2004
    231'.3—dc22   2003015778

Text Design by Meryl Sussman Levavi/Digitext

CONTENTS

✌

Preface vii

Introduction:
At the Left Hand of God xi

PART I
THE SYMBOLS OF THE SPIRIT

1. The Wind 3

2. The Fire 19

3. The Oil 35

PART II
THE MINISTRIES OF THE SPIRIT

4. Presence 53

5. Triumph 66

6. Illumination of the Word Made Print 80

7. Awakening and Evangelism 98

8. Counsel 112

PART III
THE PLEASURE OF THE SPIRIT

9. Grief 129

10. Rapture 141

11. Union with Christ 156

Notes 173

PREFACE

❧

No one should write a book merely to inform. Nor should anyone write a book to win fame or make money. Books should provide a meeting place for hungry souls to sit at a common table. The writer is expected to bring the main course, but the reader must bring the bread and wine or there will be no meal. Let us all contribute, then—writer and readers—so that, when we have said grace, we may freely invite God to join us, and our simple feast may properly begin.

I have tried in this little book to invite you, my reader, to such a table. If you want a huge and varied banquet, take a theologian to dinner. In eating with me, you will be dining only with a man who likes sitting once in a while with the Savior. Not that the Savior is uninterested in theologians! He is. But I am interested only in him. If our common meal is to become the delight I wish it to be, you must also come to the table, famished for simplicity. At the heart of your hunger will be your desire to meet with Christ, our all-important guest. Joy will be ours, for as both of us know, the Guest is even better than the meal.

His name is Jesus. He sits with us in the person of the Holy Spirit, whom I like thinking of as the "near side" of the Trinity. God the Father pervades the universe. Christ the Son stands at his right hand, having finished the work of redeeming us. The Holy Spirit is the indwelling Christ, our heart-enthroned God. But wait! Do not allow the complex mystery of the Trinity to befuddle you. Father, Son, Spirit—the three-in-one—how are we to unravel such a heady and joyous numbers game? We cannot. But we can enjoy what we could never understand. Let us enjoy God's presence, receiving it as Saint Anselm said long ago: "God is within himself a sweet society."

God's sweetness is his nearness. He sits at our table in the person of the Holy Spirit. We exult that God comes so near to us at this communion, that he actually moves inside us, making the three of us one—writer, reader, God—all in a common tryst of joy.

Let us not be quick to leave this table. After all, the Holy Spirit is here. Let us linger.

The simple food, the camaraderie of heaven—all is ours, for the great, auspicious, and terrible God is nearer than we supposed. Think of the Holy Spirit as God-at-close-range. Indwelling us, the cosmic God is ours from the inside out.

Léon Joseph Cardinal Suenens also understood the Guest to be more important than the meal. On Pentecost, 1974, he wrote:

God is here, near us, unforeseeable and loving.

I am a man of hope, not for human reasons nor from
     any natural optimism,

But because I believe the Holy Spirit is at work in the
     Church and in the world, even where his name
     remains unheard . . .

Who would dare to say that the love and imagination of
     God were exhausted?

To hope is a duty, not a luxury.[1]

Hope indeed is our duty. The Spirit is our tutor in all matters of hope. Come then. The Spirit awaits our concord. He
wants the two of us to be one. How do I know this? I just
know! He wants all things to be one. He sponsors a grand
unity of love that in its finest state permits no divisions—certainly not between writer and reader.

CALVIN MILLER
Beeson Divinity School

INTRODUCTION

AT THE LEFT HAND OF GOD

✌

And we believe in the Holy Ghost, who spake in the Law, and preached in the Prophets, and descended at Jordan, and spake in the Apostles, and indwells the Saints. And thus we believe in him, that he is the Holy Spirit, the Spirit of God, the perfect Spirit, the Spirit the Comforter, uncreated, who proceedeth from the Father, receiving of the Son, and believed on.[1]

CREED OF EPIPHANIUS
(C. A.D. 374)

Christ, according to early creeds, stands at the right of the throne of God, waiting for that moment that he will come again at times' swift end to gather us to himself. We who love him long to see him even as we sit out these impatient years of our waiting: "Even so, come, Lord Jesus" (Rev. 22:20, KJV).

But our adoration of Jesus came to us only after Christ became our Savior. It was he who called us from our focus on ourselves, enabling us to see God's agenda for our lives. Then and there, standing before Christ, we found something bigger to live for than our own petty dreams.

And who coaxed us away from our reluctance to offer him our lives? He who stands at the "left hand of God," the Holy Spirit of God. Of course, God is a spirit, having no right or left hand—but the metaphor locates the Three-in-one at the center of our daily lives.

A CALL TO VITALITY

From the outset of Christianity, the Holy Spirit summoned believers to be revolutionaries. He calls to us still, challenging us to use his power to create the Kingdom of God by transforming earth's decrepit and self-centered institutions into communities of faith and compassion.

We who love Christ either succeed or fail in direct proportion to our willingness to let the Spirit get involved in our community of faith. H. Wheeler Robinson of Oxford had to admit that in any crisis of life, only the Holy Spirit could supply him with spiritual vitality. Only the Spirit can give us real life when our physical energy flags. In his great need, he found the Holy Spirit to be a "balloon with great lifting power."[2]

The Holy Spirit is the vital center of our faith. He is also the third person of the Trinity. But to say he's third does not number his importance. We do not view him as "third," nor does that designate his numerical importance in the Trinity. He remains co-equal and co-eternal with the Father and the Son.

He is God. We must not diminish the Spirit by thinking of God as the Father, the Son and "the other one."

The Holy Spirit lives to bring God—vast as he is—within the narrow circumference of our lives. In my life, I have learned to think of him as the near side of the Trinity. God the Father pervades the universe, yet remains a holy distance from my need. God the Father is all around me—omnipresent, the theologians say. Yet for all his splendor, he rides the world on inaccessible thunderheads. Jesus, the Son, remains in heaven awaiting the grand moment of his return. But the Holy Spirit lives and walks in my small world, calling like a pleading lover to summon me to grace.

But we must be careful not to divide the Trinity into too separate forms, so separate that we imagine the three could never be one. I long ago learned to enjoy this mystery (but could never explain it). To try and pin this mystery onto any numbered definition, is like pinning down a butterfly. The definition itself destroys the grand, mysterious reality.

How can three be one? Many people try to explain the Trinity with some popular metaphors. They divide God up into three offices, if not three gods. Sabellius, a third century Christian, said that the members of the Godhead merely reflected various roles played by the same God. As an actor in a movie might play three different roles, each time on screen appearing as an entirely different character, so God, being a single actor, appeared on earth in three different forms, according to the task his role required. When God appears as Creator, we call him Father. When he appears on the stage as our Redeemer, we call him Son. When he moves into our hearts, we call him Spirit.

For years I tried to help my church members get at the

heart of this great mystery by asking them to consider the various persons of the Trinity in something like the way a chemist might examine water. At temperatures below zero Celsius, H_2O appears as a solid; at temperatures above 100 degrees Celsius, it becomes a gas (steam); and anywhere in between these two temperatures, water exists as a liquid. Nonetheless, in any of the three modes, it remains water.

Yet the attempt to assign roles to God the Father flies in the face of how we should see the Son and the Spirit. Jesus, too, was intimately involved in creation (John 1:3). The Holy Spirit, being one with the Father and Son, also played a big part in creation. Consider an early Latin hymn, *Veni Creator Spiritus*:

> Creator Spirit, by whose aid
> The world's foundations first were laid,
> Come, visit every humble mind;
> Come, pour thy joys on all mankind.[3]

At the outset of this book, we must all agree that the Holy Spirit is God the Creator, just as much as are the Father and the Son. No single member of the Trinity serves a subservient role to the other two. There is no counting up and assigning numbers—first, second or third—to any of the Trinity. They are co-equal and co-eternal.

THE PERSONHOOD OF THE SPIRIT

The Holy Spirit makes God personal to me. Who would crave the Lordship of an impersonal God? I have often sung (at least in the inner sanctum of my heart), "What a Friend I Have in

Jesus." I know that it is the Spirit who makes of Christ my inner, ever-available friend. I must confess I treasure his nearness, for when the trials of life settle upon me, I have no one to counsel me as he does. No wonder, then, that *The Message* renders 1 Corinthians 12:12, "By means of his one Spirit, we all said good-bye to our partial and piecemeal lives."

In moments of need, the grand trappings of Trinitarianism disappear in a warm togetherness that dissolves my need to understand God, even as it whets my desire to enjoy him. We are friends, the Spirit and I. Nay, more than friends—we are lovers who treasure the silence that wraps our concord. The New Testament word for the Spirit, *pneuma*, is a feminine term. This fact has led some theologians to see the Holy Spirit as feminine.[4] To any of my sisters in faith, let me say, he is surely adequate to meet all your specific feminine hungers to trust God. But for us men he is a constant companion of our own masculine way of seeing things.

For the purpose of this book, I will speak of him in the masculine as the Scripture does, and as the bulk of human history has written and thought of him. When it comes to thinking about God, it is good to use the word "him," because it harmonizes with how the Scriptures refer to God. Still, it is not good to think of God as a male. God is infinitely larger than such narrow gender assignments. One little girl wrote: "God, is it easier for men to get into heaven than women? I know you are a man, God, but try to be fair."

In this current day of utter political correctness, multiculturalists may object that it just isn't fair for God to be a man. Surely all of us would agree. To be merely a man, with all that being a "male person" implies, is to belittle God's personhood. In some ways it makes him seem inaccessible to the other half of the human race. But personhood involves other important aspects. So let us look at these personal aspects of the Godhead, particularly in relation to the personhood of the Holy Spirit.

Persons Are Emotional

I treasure the Holy Spirit, not only because he is a person, but because as a person he *feels* things. He has an emotional side. God sometimes emotes so powerfully in my own life that I can feel him within the context of my personal worship.

Revivals through the centuries have always focused on God's emotional nature. In fact, the word "ecstasy" comes into play in prominent ways in many of those times of revival. When God sweeps into the middle of our lives, we emote. We laugh, we cry, we bow, we rejoice, we are "alive in the Spirit." In fact, all things being equal, if we do not feel these things in worship, we are prone to say God is not present in our praise.

Can our worship emotions be carried to an extreme? Perhaps, but I feel most reluctant to comment on the issue. So many of my Pentecostal friends seem to have a need to feel their religion more than my Episcopal friends do. Yet I cannot castigate them for this. I suspect that how we respond to joy has much to do with the kind of personalities we have. Some souls just seem more buoyant by nature and therefore require a more demonstrative expression of their faith. To some degree, most Italians seem more jolly to me than Nordic peoples. I don't castigate either group merely for being who they are. I feel the same way about different kinds of worship styles.

Do I not have my own preferred kind of worship? Sure. I like the heritage and content of Episcopal worship. I like the open, confessional, warm style of the Assemblies of God. I feel generally happy in a Baptist church, which gives me a little of each. I often define myself as feeling most comfortable about half way between Billy Sunday and the Archbishop of Canterbury.

Remember the "Holy Laughter" movement that came out of the Toronto Revival? I never got personally involved in it, and to speak very candidly, it looked excessive to me. But at the same time, I have visited a great many dour churches where smiling seemed forbidden. There I have asked myself, "Which extreme is worse?" I do not know. At the beginning of the holy laugher revival, evangelist Rodney Howard-Browne told of a person who died of a heart attack in a "high-church" worship service. When they called in the rescue squad to carry out the poor, deceased fellow, they had to carry out three rows of dead people before locating the target corpse.

The "holy laugher" movement at least reminds us that laughter is holy and that the Holy Spirit must surely feel pleased when we delight ourselves in the presence of God. He expresses all the moods appropriate to a person.

Persons Are Communal

Each time I enter church, I remember that the Holy Spirit is the center of our community of faith. I love all those who love Christ. We exist together in close community.

Community is the preferred state of humanity. Recluses and hermits do exist in the world, but inevitably most see them as cranks and oddballs. Given the opportunity, we "normal" people avoid the sterile world of isolation. We want each other close at hand. Whether we feel happy or sad depends largely upon our ability to find a place in some community. Our mental health hinges upon community.

But we who love Christ insist that the Spirit of God be the

pillar at the center of our togetherness. In fact, we believe the Spirit is the person of the Trinity who brings us fully together to act and worship in oneness. We long to be one with Christ, but we depend upon the Spirit to make this oneness possible. When we gather, we recognize harmony as the hallmark of the Spirit. When he breathes on us, we become one in our vision and adoration. Our community grows "tight" in his presence. Our community has "communion." We are "one with" our Lord and each other—and the author of our communion is the Spirit, who erases our abrasive individualisms and pulls us into an uncanny unity.

We evangelicals often sing, *We are One in the Spirit*, or *There's a Sweet, Sweet Spirit in This Place*. We want to be one with God and with each other. The community reminds us that our foolish, selfish aloneness can accomplish little but dyspepsia and dissolution. But together we are capable of fire and force in accomplishing the purposes of God.

I remember with fondness my moderately small church in Nebraska (we had at the time about 500 members). We began to feel that God wanted us to build a new sanctuary, to be located on a new campus big enough to hold our dreams. Our people began praying and seeking God until the full weight of his glorious vision should fall fully on us. And come he did! The Spirit began to move mightily in our congregation. Not only did a large number of people join our church, but also a large number of people began making generous gifts—far beyond their means, it seemed to me. None of them was abnormally wealthy. Yet these few people raised over two and a half million dollars, merely because of the level of their sacrifices. How? They felt possessed by a dynamic oneness of community, the kind of oneness that can come only from God's Holy Spirit.

I have never felt the center of God's community so powerfully as when I visited the catacombs of Saint Sebastian in Rome. Some 525 miles of these catacombs—sunless, subterranean tubes—lace the ground beneath the city of Rome. These narrow, soft-lava passageways housed the underground community of Christians during the persecutions of Nero and later emperors. But they served as more than hideaways. They became the places where Christians gathered to cheer on their martyrs, to hold each other up in their most desperate hours. These catacombs furnished the arena of the Spirit's most important kind of community. In this space ordinary souls, who never thought of themselves as brave or valiant, suddenly found themselves in the community of the Spirit, who forged them into a union able to endure the hard times of life.

The Holy Spirit still forms the center of our best community and inflames us with a common identity and passion.

Persons Are Purposeful

Nothing can fuel the human heart once all meaning gets subtracted. We must have a purpose for life, or walk the narrow ledges of suicide or despair. Too many in the affluent west feel that they have no significant purpose for living. Many suicide notes echo this despair. "Goodbye, cruel world," often originates in a world void of purpose. The Spirit endows us with a purpose and an excitement to get the job done, and therefore ends our search for significance.

The Holy Spirit best speaks to us when we set aside time to fuel our depleted spirits with the filling presence of God. I have met many poor saints who would not appear "successful" to the world, but I have never met a single Christian who having met regularly with the Spirit felt unsure of God's purposes in life. I once visited the home of a missionary family that was achieving great things for God, yet its members seemed oddly unaware of their strategic importance to God. They did wonderful things for the poor of their parish and they were accomplishing vast things in education, medicine and Christian training—all with nothing more than their faith in God and their commitment to God's purposes. I remember the dinner they provided for my wife and me. We had scrambled eggs and dry toast. I never would have thought of serving such a meal to any of our special friends back in the United States; it would have seemed too little and unrefined. Yet here, in the presence of two committed people who always ate that way, I felt as though the Holy Spirit had directly conferred their purpose upon all of us. The Spirit operated so powerfully in their lives that their simple meal was transformed into a largesse they never saw. I found a warm mystery in their commitment that I long would celebrate. Is it possible that the Holy Spirit, in the fullness of his grace, can transform eggs into caviar?

THE MYSTERY AT THE CENTER OF TRUE FAITH

When the Holy Spirit comes in power to begin the New Testament era, as recorded in Acts 2, he arrives to the sound of rushing wind and "cloven tongues as of fire" (2:3, KJV). Later we will discuss these symbols of the Spirit (see chapters 2 and 3), but for the moment let us talk about the mystery inherent in them. If these symbols do not contain enough of the mystery of his Being, then we have only to recall that the first evidence of the Holy Spirit's presence among the disciples was their speaking in languages they had never learned.

This sign continued on through the early church. Later converts also spoke in tongues, as other places in the book of Acts record (see also 1 Corinthians 14). This phenomenon apparently broke out again at the beginning of the twentieth century with the birth of the American pentecostal movement. In the School of Biblical Studies in Topeka, Kansas, students began wondering why the "tongues" of the New Testament era no longer visited the church. Then suddenly it happened, and Agnes Ozment became the first person in modern history to have the experience.

On January 1, 1901, the Lord was present with this Kansas congregation in a new way. He brought them in touch with their hearts in order to let them focus on higher things. In the evening, near eleven o'clock, the Spirit fell on Ozment after she expressed a longing to have the congregation lay hands on her so that she might receive the gift of the Holy Spirit. As soon as the members of her church laid their hands on her head, the Holy Spirit fell on her and she began to speak in tongues, praising God. "It was," she said, "as if rivers of living water were rising up from the depths of my being."[5]

Over the next century the church became very divided over whether contemporary "tongues" (or *glossolalia*, as some spoke of them) were real languages of some sort. But one thing is for sure: the mystery of the phenomenon since then has set the Spirit in the forefront of all things vital and mystical. Perhaps it was better that the church quarrel over how the Holy Spirit did his work, rather than ignore him completely, as did so many churches of the nineteenth century.

The truth is, we all hunger for the mysterious. We know

that if God really is as great as everyone says he is, then surely he ought to be able to baffle us, at least occasionally, with things that we cannot understand. After all, such overwhelming mystery is what we most crave in religion.

I first came to faith in a Pentecostal congregation. For the first six years I was a Christian, I counted myself a Pentecostal. I feel sure that I was lured into Pentecostalism by the overwhelming joy of those who worshipped in the little church I attended. As a child I felt both baffled and intrigued by all the things my fellow worshippers said they experienced and were experiencing. People went forward claiming to be healed of dreadful things. I saw very little outward evidence for all they claimed, yet I felt most reluctant to doubt them.

And then we had speakers—evangelists, as they were called—who came to our little church to do marvelous things and to tell wondrous tales of all they had accomplished while under the spell of the Blessed Spirit. One Evangelist claimed he had spent 48 hours in hell before his brother miraculously raised him from the dead and so, lucky for him, he escaped the flames. He said he was "full of the Spirit," and it seemed to all of us that it was the Spirit who enabled him to scoot right out of the fire.

Early in my childhood faith I came to believe that all that happened was the province of the Spirit. He healed. He gave some the gift of tongues. He gave others the interpretation of tongues. I remember specific souls who seemed both vibrant and naïve. Take Sister Rogers, for example. The Holy Spirit gave Sister Rogers "the gumption to stand up to her psychiatrist." Her psychiatrist had noticed, pretty much like the rest of us, that she was paddling around with only one oar in the water. Only he told her so. According to her, the psychiatrist said to her, "Mrs. Rogers" (I remember how odd that her psychiatrist should call her "Mrs. Rogers," when everyone *knew* she was "Sister Rogers"), "if you don't give up the Holy Spirit, you are going to go crazy." To which Sister Rogers replied, partly in English and partly in tongues, "If I can go crazy for the Holy Spirit, Glory Hallellujah! *Shandala mimi, callaristo!*" Of course, we all praised the Lord right along with her, because she was finding such joy in schizophrenia. Still, as a child, I felt enthused by all the Holy Spirit seemed to be doing in lives like hers. I could tell that she knew the Holy Spirit personally with the all-pervasive force of this winning mystery of godliness.

But perhaps the most dynamic childhood image I retain of the mystery of the Holy Spirit was that of my pastor, "Sister Close." When she preached, she often seemed to be caught up in some mysterious trance. I can still remember her, leaning on the pulpit, or standing just to one side of it, rapturously looking up at the ceiling of the church as she talked to God. Only it was not so much that she looked up *at* the ceiling as she looked *through* it, right into the presence of the angels. She always spoke of the importance of being filled with the Spirit— and she seemed to me the very picture of all she taught her little flock.

In more recent years, I have preached in many third and fourth world countries. Among the poor I have discovered what Jesus meant when he named as one sign of his Messiahship that "the poor have the gospel preached to them" (Matt. 11:5, KJV). In desperately poor countries of this world, all that many Christians own is the good news. They have no "things," no real estate or autos. So they cherish Christ. Naturally, they take their religion seriously.

The Holy Spirit is the center of all they are. His presence in their midst is, for them, wealth immeasurable. And he acts!

When the only riches to be had are the wealth of God's presence, godliness still walks the earth. Those filled with the Spirit are made rich with realities that the materially rich could never fathom.

THE SOURCE OF VITALITY FOR ALL FAITH

In the last decade or so, Americans have fallen away from church attendance by a factor of twelve percent. I visit a lot of churches and it often seems to me that I see a lot more non-vital churches than I did a decade ago. Churches seem largely void of the mystery that only God can supply through the ministry of the Holy Spirit.

The late Christian educator Findley Edge said thirty years ago that people would endure anything in religion except the absence of vitality. If vitality is the gift of the Holy Spirit, then Dr. Edge must have been saying that people will not long endure worship where there is no evidence of the Holy Spirit's involvement. We must have mystery to live. We must have mystery to experience the vitality of God's involvement in our praise.

And why do so few churches evidence this vitality? Ministers are better educated than ever before. We have the finest technical support, PowerPoint presentations, and imported music. Yet in spite of this, people in ever-increasing numbers are staying home from church.

I am convinced that the world is looking for the kind of vitality not to be had in the mere hype that has taken the place of the Spirit in so many evangelical churches. We are too hungry for the eternal to feel satisfied with the contrived and the contemporary.

When the Spirit comes, we no longer resist long worship services. We cannot stay long enough. In his presence we scorn to leave church too soon, for we might miss the next glorious miracle the Spirit brings to all his enthralled lovers. It is hard to predict exactly where or when his spell might fall upon us, but it always feeds on two or three simplicities.

First, he comes upon those who hunger for an affair with Christ. The Holy Spirit is in business for Jesus. He comes upon all those who seek the Savior and who crave his inwardness.

Second, he prefers a confessional and honest atmosphere. During any period of revival, the Spirit prompts a confessional worship atmosphere.

Third, and most important, he comes to those who seek to yield to his love and demands. This means that the vision, which the Holy Spirit longs to confer, waits primarily because he seeks those who eagerly make obedience their passion.

So here at the outset of this book, let us rejoice! God, the Holy Spirit, is in league with God the Father and God the Son—and therefore we do not have to make our way upon the planet alone.

PART I

THE
SYMBOLS
OF THE
SPIRIT

❧

1

THE WIND

It takes a breeze to make a banner speak! . . .
Terra came alive and people ran into the streets
To feel the water and the wind.
None were ashamed to see themselves soaked in
   blinding, driving rain.
It was the changing of the age.[1]

CALVIN MILLER

The wind brings all things. It is the mother of rain and the father of weather. It is the dance of new air that washes the blasting drought. It is invisible and powerful, beyond the senses and real. The wind is the soul of nature. Few things in this world can serve as a symbol of the Spirit, for most things are either too visible, too touchable or too stationary.

The wind, therefore, is the Bible's most moving metaphor for the Spirit of God.

How Real Is It?

Who can doubt the vitality of wind? Who can measure it in any concrete way? We cannot see it. Yet it flies at us, whispering its substance in the breeze, shouting its soul in the gales. It challenges us to define its existence as it sweeps over us in its subtle and elusive forms, making life possible.

Just how real is it?

Recently a friend of mine flew me from Tampa to Birmingham in his private plane. "The wind," he said, "is blowing directly toward us as we fly and it is coming at a force of thirty knots. Whatever speed the air speed indicator tells us we are going, we must subtract thirty knots." I found this a marvel that we had to reckon with something so totally invisible yet something that could not be discounted. It was there to say, "Here I am, a mystery beyond you with which you must reckon as you compute your travel time. You will not arrive as early as you might if you did not have to reckon with me. I am a real but invisible force."

I remember an odd day in 1975 in Omaha, Nebraska, where I served as pastor. I had turned on the television just in time to hear the announcer warn me of a tornado coming my way. I remember thinking, *How odd that the weatherman could pinpoint my very street and neighborhood.* I knew he was talking about me. I walked to the kitchen window just in time to see the roof lift off the house behind ours. I have never been able to shake the odd sensation. It felt so surreal! I stood in the wake of a casual wind, when the breeze twisted into violence and I watched the shingled roof of the house behind me lift and hang for a moment in thin air before it floated upward and shuddered into nothingness.

Wind is only air in motion, yet it symbolizes the invisible reality and power of God. How well does the symbol serve?

Here and there I have visited a worship service where the ordinary Sunday words suddenly wrapped themselves in heavy expectancy. The air that had seemed immobile and dead began to stir. With a force unexplainable, it then flew at us and we became more than we were. The mystery hung all about us. Heavy, crushing things were lifted. Our reluctance to love God dissolved. We became more than we ever thought we could be. Our passion for God became a violent headwind, a whirlwind, a God-sent tornado of force. The Spirit came with an invisible force both glorious and transforming.

What is to be said of this glorious Spirit, this Wind incomparable? Let us journey into the heart of the Spirit's mighty metaphor of transformation and power.

OF PNEUMA, PNEO, RUACH, SPIRIT

The words commonly used for Spirit in the Bible also convey the ideas of wind or breath. This is true in both the Old Testament (Hebrew, *ruach*) and the New Testament (Greek, *pneuma*). The Latin verb *spiro*, out of which we derive the word Spirit, also carries the idea of breathing. From this same Latin word we derive terms like *inspire* (to breath into) or *respire* (to breathe).

Small wonder that when Jesus gives the Spirit to the apostles in the Book of John, he breathes on these gallant souls and says to them, "Receive the Holy Spirit" (John 20:22, NIV). I use the word "breathe" as a kind of prayer. I must have this breath of Christ to live. Any day that God's Spirit does not breathe in my life is a wasted day. I love it most when I enjoy constant renewal, so I pray unceasingly the words of a hymn from my childhood:

> Holy Spirit, breathe on me,
> Until my heart is clean.
> Let sunshine fill my inmost part,
> With not a cloud between.

Of all the "breathe" words that most intrigue me, the Hebrew word for breath fascinates me most. *Ruach* can mean wind, breath or Spirit.

The Hebrews had a covenant name for God: Yahweh, or as they generally spelled it, YHWH (since they did not write out the vowels of their alphabet). This word YHWH, their earliest and most important word for God, is a breathy kind of word with a touch of onomatopoeia about it. Onomatopoeia is a type of word that sounds like that which it defines. Bees *buzz*, for instance; the word *buzz* describes what bees do by sounding like what they do.

Some suggest that YHWH, this very breathy word for God, comes to us as a form of onomatopoeia. In the nomadic phase of their civilization, the Hebrews lived mostly outside. They heard God in the elements. He ordered them forward in thunder, in the blistering heat of Sinai or the desert storms. And always there was the wind, moaning at midnight around their fragile tents, coming in siroccos from the desert or in whirlwinds of destruction. They felt both its desert threat and cooling bliss, and yet it remained invisible to them. It seems natural that the wind, during their nomadic years, might become their word for God.

While *ruach*, unlike YHWH, is not onomatopoeiac, it does refer to the force of YHWH so often symbolized by the wind. It may be only the power of suggestion, but when I see God, as *Ruach*, moving in powerful ways in the Asian countries where I travel, I have only to close my eyes and let the ears of my heart serve. When I do this, I am convinced I hear the roar of wind, the *Ruach*, sent as the renovating gales of YHWH.

I first experienced this phenomenon in a crowded Beijing house church. While I prayed in a sweltering room packed with Chinese believers, the press of the crowd seemed chaotic. We had no air conditioning and the doors and windows had to be shut up for fear that our hymns and prayers would be heard and reported to the police. Just when I thought I would pass out because of the heat, I felt a strange sense of wind, a ventilation of the heart, the *Ruach*, the *Pneuma*, the breath of God. And wonderful things soon unfolded.

Israel knew this same *Ruach*. She believed in the one YHWH, an omnipotent, all-pervasive, breathing *Ruach* God. He was not like the masculine he-gods of the pagan nations. The Hebrew God was too real, too invisible, too all-pervasive to take any tangible, sculpted form. Their God was a Spirit who came like the wind with all of his attributes and blessings—his elusive reality, his sudden gentility, his towering threats.

In the New Testament, Jesus says to Nicodemus, "The wind (*pneo*) bloweth where it listeth, and thou hearest the sound thereof, but canst not tell whence it cometh, and whither it goeth: so is every one that is born of the Spirit" (*pneuma*, John 3:8, KJV).

The similarities between wind and breath are not so unthinkable as it might at first seem. In ancient times, most people lived life outdoors. Those who spend much time in the open inevitably build a huge awareness of God (outdoors has never been the friend of atheism). God was open space, geographical vastness. He was all skyscape, oceanscape, landscape. The wind became the voice of God—God himself. Job's God came to him in the whirlwind and spoke to him from a tornado. A tempest-driven leviathan devoured Jonah. The fierce winds of the Mediterranean sent Paul into his near-fatal ordeal of shipwreck.

WIND, THE SYMBOL OF DELIVERANCE

> Then Moses stretched out his hand over the sea; and the
> LORD swept the sea back by a strong east *ruach* all night
> (Ex. 14:21, NASB).

I have always considered the Exodus in the Old Testament to be roughly the equivalent of the Cross in the New Testament. In this wonderful picture of redemption, Moses calls on God and God shows up in the form of a redeeming wind. With apocalyptic force, the wind holds back the watery walls of the Red Sea, the people pass through the sea and are saved. So the Bible gives the wind credit for this wonderful miracle of salvation.

Some might ask, how could a wind strong enough to hold back the waters of the Red Sea not also hold back the Israelites from passing through it? This worthy question presents us with a paradox, like many other miracles of Scripture. It's difficult to understand. But for our purposes, the important issue here is that the Bible credits the wind for the miracle.

I have often felt this breath of God, and to know it even for a single second is to crave it forever. Each time I have felt the wind, I long to know the renovation and change it brings to the heart of Christ's church. I have seen the same Wind of Pentecost that first came as a symbol of the Spirit. Wind symbolizes revolution and new beginnings. We often speak of "the winds of change." The best of my sermons ring with a passion derived from the blowing of this Wind. It is a creation passion that creates the church as surely as it created the universe in Genesis 1.

As I wrote earlier, I spent much of my young years attending the sermons of Oklahoma evangelists. The Wind of their godly passion enthralled us. We wept when they led us in weeping; we laughed when they led us in laughter. These masters of the human nervous system caused us to feel what they felt. And while I do not exalt emotion as the god of worship, feeling is not all bad. Emotion in some ways indicates that the Wind of God is blowing.

In planting a church, I grew addicted to feeling the winds of conversion. When the Wind blew, people in the throes of divorce came full circle to marital health. Belligerent and rebellious and dysfunctional children found themselves transformed. These radical changes brought great joy. Certainly, emotion can be overdone. Emotion for emotion's sake soon goes flat. But when it comes as evidence that God is reclaiming and reshaping his world, how welcome it should be!

I have come to see healthy emotion as a sign of life in the church. It often gives the most obvious evidence that God is really involved. Far too often in these latter days I come and go in church without feeling a thing. I remain captive to the mass analgesia, the mass anesthesia, and the mass amnesia. The analgesia reminds me that many sermons feel nearly painful. The anesthesia speaks of their power to drug the vitality of faith. The amnesia suggests that they are eminently forgettable.

Still, when the church came alive in Acts 2, emotion ran high. Observers accused the believers of drunkenness because they seemed joyous to a fault. And how welcome the emotion was! It symbolized the church had been made new and was about to bring even more renovation to its needy world.

It probably is not a sign of health that no one any longer accuses the church of being drunk. We have traded the heady exhilaration of the Spirit for sluggish sermons and yawning hymns.

Wind, the Hovering Symbol of Creation

> And the earth was without form and void; and darkness was upon the face of the deep. And the spirit of God moved upon the face of the waters (Gen. 1:2, KJV).

This verse describes the creation as a watery chaos confronted by the Wind of God. The verse could just as adequately read, *The Wind of God began to move upon the face of the waters.* The Wind here broods like a hen over an unhatched cosmos, waiting to see what this unformed universe will hatch. It is the brooding Wind that sits and moves and hatches and gives life. The Wind becomes the hovering symbol of creation.

In a loftier and more personal sense, the Spirit now hovers over prodigal and useless lives to transform them into servants and ministers. The Holy Spirit is ever creating and recreating us in the likeness of Christ, as the Wind of the Spirit begins to blow.

Philippians 2:5 exhorts us to have the mind of Christ. Now minds and brains are not the same things (all of us know people who have the one and don't seem to have the other), but if we take Paul seriously here, we must think of the brain as the vehicle and the mind as the driver.

Brains operate at various speeds. When the brain oscillates at 5-8 cycles per second, the Theta state, the person who owns that brain is driving very slow indeed. In fact, 5-8 cycles per second probably indicates that the owner of that brain is comatose and very near to death. When the brain speeds up to 9-14 cycles per second, the Alpha state, the person is enjoying some healthy sleep. When the brain speeds up to 15-40 cycles per second, the Beta state, the person has reached a state of creative rest. The Beta state is true Sabbath. We are in his presence and at peace. Here we are so "with God" that our conversation with him is entire. We are in rapt oneness with God. Artists create best with the mind at rest, allowing them to access their most creative talents. In this Beta state sculptors sculpt, painters paint, and poets exude odes and sonnets.

But the Beta state has an even greater attribute. In this state of mind we are most apt to enter into reverent contemplation of the Spirit of God. In other words, here is where the Wind blows, and the Spirit comes to help us create even as we worship. Here is true *inspiration* (and remember, the word inspiration is the Latin equivalent of the Greek word, *pneuma*), in which the ability to create is breathed into us. Here God creates beauty through us, by the same principle of "inbreathing" he has always used to make his world and his saints more like himself.

WIND, A SYMBOL OF LIFE COMING

> And the LORD God formed man of the dust of the ground,
> and breathed into his nostrils the breath of life; and man be-
> came a living soul (Gen. 2:7, KJV).

If the wind symbolizes the coming of creation, in salvation it
certainly symbolizes the coming to life. In this passage the
word *ruach* once again is used as the breath or wind of life.
God calls humankind into existence by the blessed coming of
the wind. The breath of God creates life. How consistent is this
image of wind with that of the Spirit!

African lore teaches that all lion cubs are born dead. They
would remain that way, except that the Great Lion King of the
Jungle comes and breathes into the dead cubs' nostrils the
breath of life and so the cubs begin to live. This picture faintly
echoes the *ruach* of Genesis 2:7. The newly created Adam is
lifeless, and only the breath of God can call him to life. And so
the breath of God does exactly that.

The same thing can be said of the breath (the *ruach*) as it
calls the dead of Ezekiel 37 to life. The prophet sees a large valley in which heaps of dry bones have come together to form a
vast sea of skeletons. God asks Ezekiel, "Son of man, can these
bones live?" (v. 3) Then as the winds of God begin to blow,
flesh covers the skeletons. Yet they remain breathless corpses.

"Then he said unto me, Prophesy unto the *ruach*, prophesy, son of man, and say to the *ruach*, Thus sayeth the LORD
God; Come from the four winds, O breath, and breathe upon
these slain, that they may live" (v. 9, KJV). At the word of the
prophet, the bones begin to live. The Wind ever brings the life.

One of Paul's contemporaries was a man named Apollos.

Like many modern preachers, Apollos saw little evidence of the life-creating *pnuema* or *ruach* in his ministry. He preached to great crowds who seemed enthusiastic about his sermons, but his words lacked real life because they were void of the Holy Spirit. In Acts 19:1–2 Paul asked some of Apollos' confused converts if they had received the Holy Spirit since they believed. After sitting under Apollos' sermons, his disciples felt baffled by the term "the Holy Spirit." They had never heard the words. Second Corinthians already had been written by then, but apparently Apollos had not taken the time to read it. (Reading seems not to have been his forte.) But there it was— I Corinthians 2:12: "We have not received the spirit of the world but the Spirit who is from God, that we may understand what God has freely given us." (NIV) Apollos' sermons neither invoked nor experienced the Holy Spirit—the changing Wind of God.

Are American preachers serving the Wind of Acts 2? In most cases, it seems not so. It has been years since George Barna gave us a picture of what Americans think of American preachers:

Only 51 percent of evangelicals think they hear excellent preaching.

Only 42 percent of mainline denominationalists think their preacher is excellent.

Only 34 percent of Catholics think so.[2]

Ian Pitt-Watson once said, *Predicatio Verbi Dei est Verbum Dei*—"The preaching of the words of God is the Word of God."[3] Who can deny it? So to stand in a holy moment and speak what God wants said is to wear the prophet's mantle.

I am convinced that while most people don't know how to clearly articulate what they want out of church. If they could put it into words, they would say that they long to feel the force of an Acts 2 Wind. They want Christ to permeate the sermon because already he has so permeated the life of the preacher. We cannot get Christ in the sermon by consciously working at upping the word count of the name "Jesus." No, the issue of sermonic power is far simpler than that. The preacher must hunger for Jesus. When the preacher gets hungry for Jesus, the hunger of those who come to church will automatically be sated.

Unfortunately, Apollos still lives. He thrives. The absence of the Spirit in our sermons should embarrass us. In the hunger for something substantial, the Apollos School of Homiletics has brought to pass the chilling words of Amos:

> "The days are coming," declares the sovereign LORD,
> "when I will send a famine through the land—
> not a famine for food or a thirst for water,
> but a famine of hearing the words of the LORD.
> Men will stagger from sea to sea and wander from north
> to east . . .
> but they will not find it" (Amos 8:11–12, NIV).

There exists one valid question for anybody's church: "Have you received the Holy Spirit since you believed?" How can we tell whether the Holy Spirit is present? Well, who can describe every aspect of the way he works?

When the Spirit first came in Acts, his coming seemed to be marked by a kind of madness, of babbling in languages the Jews had never learned and acting rather like they were drunk. Perhaps they were—inebriated by the Spirit. Paul summons us to such intoxication when he says, "And be not drunk with wine, wherein is excess; but be filled with the Spirit" (Eph. 5:18, KJV).

Heady inebriation, this Spirit intoxication! I find it a most glorious addiction. One sip and I am a *pneumaholic* who must have more of the *Pneuma*! I may not be wholly doctrinal or crisply theological, but I am alive and my life is in the Wind, Wind that blows to disorient my propriety. This Wind scatters the paper trails of my lifeless way of life and my empty ambitions. One of the evidences of the Spirit's presence is what might be called the coming of a glorious chaos!

Remember that in the aftermath of any wind comes chaos. But in the church, chaos may actually be a life sign. The life of the Wind is rarely in things well ordered. Programs and organizing are not necessarily signs of life. The Wind brings things too glorious to be organized. And this Wind is the crying need of churches that think they can organize their way to success. Overplanning may be a symptom of decay, not of health. Chaos—when God flies at us too fast to measure or structure—may be a symptom of vitality. How extensive is this chaos of glory!

I will long remember a service in a small church in Benaue of the Philippines. At the conclusion of the meeting, forty or fifty people crowded forward to the altar. The pastor and I were the only counselors. I felt smothered by the chaos of those desiring healing and those seeking a new life in Christ. One man asked me to pray for his healing—something foreign to my denominational experience. But in the madness of so many, and being driven by the Spirit, I prayed for his healing. I don't know if he was healed, but the light in his face following my prayer told me that prayer itself is a kind of healing.

Two hours later, I had to admit that I had never seen anything so glorious or so chaotic.

Think of the aftermath of Peter's sermon in Acts 2. Three thousand people cried out to be saved! The population of the church grew from 120 members to three thousand in thirty minutes' time. The baptism service must have lasted far into the night! But then, the church is most remarkable when the glory is too vast to organize. This is one of the most powerful evidences that God is involved, when circumstances move too fast to be organized. Such events mark the nearness of his presence—the nearness of the *pneuma*, the *ruach*, the Wind of God.

In every great awakening when the Wind begins to blow, participants feel the event is too real to leave. People arrive early and stay late. God, who has never been to them as interesting as their culture, becomes all-enthralling. They want him, crave him, and the Wind brings a refreshing to the deserts they foolishly once called worship. And so they forsake that dead togetherness they mislabeled "joy" when they remained more in charge of things.

JESUS AND NICODEMUS AND THE WIND OF MYSTERY

When Jesus calls on Nicodemus in John 3, the Master likens the Holy Spirit to the wind. Listen to his key phrases: "The wind blows wherever it pleases. You hear its sound, but you cannot tell where it comes from or where it is going" (John 3:8, NIV). In this passage, Jesus uses the symbol of wind to speak of the mystery of God. While we alluded to this in the introduction, we must pass the truth once again. Without this incredible mystery, the church loses the spell of her intrigue. People feel drawn to this intrigue. Like the tractor beam of a *Star Trek* spaceship, we find ourselves drawn into the arena of his activity.

The new literature of church growth often counsels us to believe that churches grow when congregations become public relations experts. We have only to smile incessantly and pump a few hands, and presto! Mega-church! Everyone on the church staff is encouraged to keep smiling and shake as many hands as possible. We believe that when we get good enough at public relations, the church will grow. This bears some truth, but it is weak truth. When churches grow only because of their "let's be the friendliest place in town" mystique, it is weak growth indeed—a pitifully weak substitute for the involvement of the Spirit.

When churches grow because those who attend feel spellbound by the mystery of things they cannot understand, however, the church is impelled toward glory and it grows with an otherworldly vitality. And that sort of vitality is the only kind that counts.

Years ago I found myself in bed one late Sunday midnight, just lying there, looking up at the ceiling and smiling. I asked myself the reason for this stupidity. The only answer that came to me was that I had been smiling all day, and this was the most reasonable thing I could do. I just couldn't stop smiling, since I had been doing it all day long. I was doing it out of some notion—false indeed—that if I smiled enough, the church would grow. In my own mind, *I* was the source of good times and sweet rapport. How much I had to learn!

Unless the Spirit provides this intrigue and warmth, we create only bogus hype.

LET US WELCOME THE WIND

The wind is the symbol of God the Holy Spirit. All that is vital relates to that Wind. All that is Holy. All that is mystery and intrigue.

It is time that we welcome the Wind. It is time that we seek a vital chaos! Only then may we sing the anthem of the church's continuance in the world:

> Breathe on me, breath of God,
> Till I am all thine own,
> Until my will is lost in thine,
> To live for thee alone.

2

THE FIRE

Praise to you
Spirit of fire!
to you who sound the timbrel
and the lyre.
Your music sets our minds ablaze![1]

HILDEGARD OF BINGEN

Mary Skobtsova died in a Nazi gas chamber during Lent of 1945. Had she lived another day, allied invaders would have liberated her. But she had committed her life to a much higher flame than that of Auschwitz. She loved Christ and served the Spirit and cried out the theme of her life, "Lord, I am your messenger. Throw me like a blazing torch into the night."[2] Mary's cry for fire reflects the incendiary symbol of God's Spirit.

Fire is the symbol of purification, renovation, and change.

Fire is the emblem of the Spirit. It is God's unquenchable heat sent to warm the iciest of human circumstances.

It is the torch of heaven—a flame set next to the arctic of our selfish reluctance to enjoy the will of God.

It is a visible light to illumine the direction that God has set for us in this world.

There is no fire like Spirit fire. Nothing can empower the church like the incendiary joy of Acts 2. Yet this flame eludes us. While no one could ever understand this searing mystery of the Spirit, a fire burns in every person with an appetite for faith.

HUNGER FOR FIRE

Here and there in life I have felt the gales of Acts 2 blow freely on my soul. Frequently, yet too infrequently, I have seen the dancing flame. But I know its addiction, for having seen it once, I would see it more and more.

I know all too well this hunger for the fire. I want to feel the warmth of God. I want it to drive my service for Christ. I want it to whet my desire to know there exists a reality unseen by those who never suspect my hunger.

I have a friend roughly my age. When we were both young pastors, the wildfire of God seared his ministry, sweeping up his church in the magnificence of revival. Then the elusive flame flickered and cooled. Thereafter his ministry, though vital, lived haunted by the notion that the best visits of God had ceased. This all happened more than forty years ago now. He has since lived out these decades with a supreme yearning for that fire to return. It never has. Who can say if it ever will?

As we have grown older, I have noticed in him an odd

vacuum of hope. He has a restless appetite to fill himself once again with that same Presence that once possessed his congregation. I have counseled him to remain faithful and not become so dissolute over his yearning, for such fire may never again come as it did during his younger ministry. But he cannot forget and will not lay by his desire to have it all happen again. He remembers and he ever reaches backward to try and regain that dissipated glory.

All of my life, I have served in a denomination that teaches the importance of a Spirit-filled ministry. All of my life I have lived among ministers hungry for the fire of God to fall. Often—very often—I have lived among those who cried out for the fire. But in most cases when God gives the fire, it has not come in response to people asking for fire. Fire seems to be the by-product of what the best people crave. Want fire and you get nothing. Want God with all your heart and the fire will be yours without the asking.

I learned this in 1960 through a 70-year-old missionary who had served for forty-five years in Argentina. This sometime prayer partner taught me of Christ not by cold theological precepts, but by example. I never heard her ask God for any evidence of his reality. But in every prayer she begged God to give her more of himself. She had fire in her life continually—fire to accomplish all God wanted done. Yet never once did she ask God for it. Always she begged God for his presence. Thus she never needed to ask for fire.

Let us return to the day of Pentecost in Acts 2. Notice the despair of the waiting disciples. They feel destroyed in heart by the absence of Jesus who has just returned to the Father. How they long to see him and know him first hand once again! This longing after Christ manifests itself in ten days of waiting prayer that raises their ardor and passion for his presence. Then, when their prayers for his presence reach fever pitch, the fire falls.

This is no mystery. Fire is always God's reply to a hunger for his presence. These flame-visited disciples, like my senior missionary prayer partner, did not pray for fire. They prayed for his presence and got the fire.

But perhaps it is worth noting the shape of the fire that appeared on people's heads in Acts 2. It came in "cloven tongues of flame." In some ways this is an unremarkable description of fire, since fire quite often appears as tongues of flame. But many Bible scholars believe that the description of "tongues" is meant to describe what happened to a Christian witness as a result of the Spirit's coming. For the tongues of these disciples were set loose in the world to inform the world of the coming of Christ. These "tongues" symbolized the primary method of evangelism: the preaching of the gospel.

THE FIRE OF CLEANSING AND PURIFICATION

The evangelist, Charles Finney, wrote of his conversion this way:

> There was no light in the room, nevertheless, it appeared to me as if it were perfectly light. As I went in and shut the door after me, it seemed to me as if I met the Lord Jesus Christ face to face. It did not occur to me then nor did it for some time afterwards, that it was a wholly mental state. On the contrary it seemed to me that I saw him as I would see any other man. He said nothing, but looked at me in such a manner as to break me right down at his feet . . . it

seemed to me a reality that he stood before me and I fell down at his feet and poured out my soul to Him. I wept aloud like a child, and made such confessions as I could with a choked utterance. It seemed to me that I bathed his feet with tears, and yet I had no distinct impression that I touched him.[3]

Finney spoke of no light, and yet spoke of the room as perfectly lit. This is the mystery of the Spirit's fire. Is it literal, or is it ethereal? Is it oxidation (the chemical definition of physical fire), or is it completely real and yet a complete mystery?

It is ethereal fire, yet God sends this flame to do the real work of cleansing and purification. Take Sodom and Gomorrah, for instance. These cities needed the flame to help them clean up their act, only their act had at last gotten so bad, that the amount of fire needed to cleanse their cities did away with their cities.

Fire is the great purgative. The last time the bubonic plague hit a European city, fire ended its terror. The story goes that the great fire of London in 1665 halted the plague—the flame that Londoners so lamented as accidental and a horror. Yet this fire brought the very purgation the city needed to end the contagion. This is a healthy way to look at the flame of God as it burns through human willfulness to make a place for a morally cleansed globe. Such a cleansing gets us ready for the coming of God in the world.

"Purging" fire supplies the basis of our word *purgatory*. Purgatory has for its chief idea, cleansing. In the Roman Catholic sense, it is a cleansing from all unconfessed, venial sins. This is the flame of a temporary hell that burns to clean. Once purged, the poor sufferer can proceed to heaven.

But is purging the real meaning of Holy Spirit Fire? I believe it is. The Greek word for fire is *pyr*, most often pronounced *pur*. The word forms the linguistic basis of the popular heat-resistant glass called *Pyrex*. It also supplies the root of a great many other words: purgation, purgatory, purging, pyromania, etc. But the word as it appears in Acts functions not so much as a concept as a symbol. As a symbol, it gives light and cleanliness and power to the church. This *pyr* comes from God to purify and cleanse and get the world ready for the coming of holiness and the firestorm of God's saving love.

THE FIRE OF WARMTH IN RELATIONSHIPS

This fire is the soul of warm relationships. As such, the fire has little interest in "churchy propriety." This fire ends in joy, and joy tends to result in delirium when it reaches its most intoxicating high. This is why observers accused the first disciples in Acts of public drunkenness. Yet the "high" we experience tends toward excesses that we never would have known had we stuck to our concerns about looking proper.

If the Spirit has taught me anything, it is that propriety is overrated. Some years ago in Costa Rica I preached in two very different congregations. The morning service, I preached in a Baptist church that had been "denominationalized" by my own very proper group. The few who attended, dressed just like their American missionaries and mentors had taught them to: suit and ties, hats and gloves, starchy shirts and even starchier liturgy. The singing sounded thin and dull, all done according to a printed order of worship, neatly typed . . . and never disturbed by any breath of spontaneity. Proper! Properly dull! Properly dead!

That night I preached in an old movie theater, taken over for "the work of Jesus" by Pentecostals. The nursery overflowed with beautiful little brown babies crammed in playpens all in the same room with the rest of us. They toddled, cried and laughed while in the old, torn theater seats just ahead of them, the rest of us worshipped and tried to drown out their noise with a joyful noise of our own. It was all improper—improper but vitally improper! It was dry kindling before the fire, unhindered by liturgical Greek or Hebrew or anything Latinesque. The fire came!

This "propriety versus impropriety" conundrum haunts me. I do not want to abandon impropriety until my excesses make me appear more athletic than authentic. In 1 Corinthians 14:23 Paul expresses a concern that the joy that issues in speaking in tongues may cause an uninformed world to criticize the church and its ill treatment of mystery. Nevertheless, the mystery the world wants to find may be obscured by my desire for stiff propriety. I suppose I had rather risk a little "wildfire" than feel no fire at all. Nonetheless, excess should be kept within control. Most people want to enjoy God without fearing the bizarre behavior of over-happy Christians who make their private psychosis a requirement for going to church.

Joy makes the church credible for me. I will talk later about the Spirit as the fulfillment of God's presence in his church. But I must say one thing here: when the Spirit is present, I find myself open to joy. Joy, as one early Christian martyr reminds us, provides proof of the presence of God.

Are there not times when the church must be serious and devout? Of course. Are there not times when the church must commiserate with brothers and sisters who endure times of untold agony or personal pain? Are there not times when the church, like any family, becomes dysfunctional—firing staff members, getting locked in quarrels, dividing and dissolving in disruption and hate? Yes, to be sure. Still, the most obvious sign of health in a church is when God is alive at the center of a loving community, warmed by the fires of the Holy Spirit.

In this sense, warmth indicates life itself. Many things distinguish a living person from a corpse, but body temperature provides one sure-fire difference. A measurement of 98.6 degrees gives the person a better chance of health and life than a lower reading.

Sometimes the mood of the nation filters into the community of God with an icy blast of almost devastating force. Who can forget 9/11? I remember preaching on those Sundays when the force of national shock and grief hit every person present. But I also will never forget how the churches I attended during those weeks of pain seemed caught up in a time of bright confidence that God still remained in charge of history. During those weeks, more than ever, I felt the fullness of God. At that time of suffering the church gave the Holy Spirit his best leeway, and the room he received allowed him to bring a kind of fire that many churches hadn't seen for a long time.

Suffering brings on a crying need for the fire. When I writhe in the flame of my own despair, I am most likely to feel the flame of God's purgation or victory. The world is like a Rembrandt painting, a play of light and darkness. Claudel said: "Jesus did not come to explain suffering nor to take it away: he came to fill it with his presence."[4]

How true! "Every Suffering is He," wrote Chiara Lubich.[5]

I was serving in one church just outside New York, shortly after 9/11. The skies still burned, the smoke still rolled, but the urban grief in its own way made a place for God. While the weeping seemed greater and the laughter more rich with purpose, the thing I really noticed was that people unaccustomed to hugging suddenly felt less fond of propriety than before. It was as if the Christians of a whole nation were attending the funeral of the same loved one. We grieved together, laughed together. God had set a fire loose in our pro-American midst, and the fire brought real warmth.

We welcomed this warmth in such a cold time. We needed a little fire. People turned to God, and in those churches wise enough to know the heat of the Spirit, a kind of fire blazed a path for new converts to come to faith in Christ. Baptisms became frequent and the national spirit confessed its need of the Holy Spirit.

But the ardor cooled all too soon. The fire soon dissipated. Even the aisles grew cold. We feared that if we granted the fire too much space, it would devour our common sense and we would do something so incredibly Pentecostal that we would look like those on the most excessive kind of cable television religious orgies. So, given the poles of Pentecostalism and Episcopalianism, we had rather side with those whose propriety is frozen than those who have lost all decorum.

In the movie, *Somewhere in Time*, the female protagonist says that the key to great acting is to prevent the role from becoming "hammy" by keeping the "excess within control." This has been our usual approach to the Spirit's involvement in our lives. We want to shut him down, lest he become too involved and we see his drama degenerate into an emotive firestorm of drivel. We all want to serve the flames but cage the fire in our own little denominational incinerators of ordered religion. We would rather gag in the smoke than allow ourselves the pleasure of the fire.

We sin by making propriety the god that kills all vitality.

I remember my mother becoming miffed with us on more than one occasion because we children were having too good a time and making too much noise. Yet mother often lost in this matter. For once the giggles had broken loose, it was impossible to contain them. When mother became irate and threatened us, we would clamp our mouths shut until the inner force of the giggles burst forth, causing us to risk our lives—for our mother was a strict disciplinarian. But often mother sensed our pain and broke into laughter with us. What a great relief! Mother did not punish us; she joined with us! This welcome joy kindled the bright fire of family relationships.

This must be the way our heavenly Father feels about the falling of the fire of the Spirit. In the case of our family, our outburst of giggles may not have been the best time to measure our mental health—but it was the best time to measure the health of our family. Fire, when freely welcomed in a church, gives the world the best picture of church health.

BAPTISM, A SYMBOL OF POWER TO GET THINGS DONE

Dunamis, the Greek word for power (the term that furnishes us with the root of the English word *dynamite*), appears often in the New Testament. *Dunamis* is a word of explosive power. It is the dynamite of God. I see this dynamite in my life and in the lives of others when God is called upon to demolish all barriers of offense that exist between us and him.

I like thinking about the building of the first railway

across America. Most people only vaguely remember that the section of the Union Pacific railroad between Omaha and Provo, Utah—where the two sections of transcontinental track joined—took only half the time required to build the section between San Francisco and Provo. And yet the western leg of the railroad stretched only half the distance of the eastern half. Why the discrepancy? The short 500 miles of the western half had to cross the Sierras and the Rockies. These formidable mountain barriers had to be blasted into tunnels that permitted the rails to pass.

And what made the railroad possible? Dynamite! Workers first made a small cavern in the granite heart of a mountain, then filled that chamber with dynamite. Next they blocked the entrance and laid the wick. Then they lit the wick and a flash of fire traveled sometimes a long distance back to the heart of the mountain. Finally the earth trembled and shuddered and the barriers gradually dissolved before the power of *dunamis* fire.

Sometimes the barriers we face leave us feeling jailed in a prison of our own making, with no way out. Do not believe it. The Holy Spirit is still the dynamite of God!

FIRE AS THE ENERGY OF THE KINGDOM

Nothing provides a more heady image of revival or awakening than fire, out of control, driven by the wind and driving maddened cobras ahead of it.

I have seldom read a more powerful secular novel than Richard Adams's *Shardik*. He tells of a great bear, fleeing a forest fire and crashing into the world of terrified villagers. Anyone who has read the opening pages of his novel feels forever locked in the spell of this scene. Shardik, this great beast, this symbol of the incarnation of Christ, breaks through the burning forest, crashing through the fire in a Vesuvius of hot, white sparks. Shardik presages the fire of apocalypse to announce the last days. And fire is the ensign.

Still, the villagers in Adams's novel all too soon make a god of the bear. They put him in a cage to worship him, in much the same way that we try to box God in Gothic buildings and then order him to empower us with a freedom we have not given him. Little good ever comes from packaging the God of fire. The tighter our organizational box, the less fire we may expect. We domesticate God, then demand he be feral. We slick God up in altar lace and then order him to look manly. We become fascinated with the God of theology only to lose the God of fire. Remember that T. H. White said of Guinevere that she was wild about theology, but had never much cared for God.

Just after the turn of the twentieth century, Evan Roberts came to Laughor, Wales. He began entering into long periods of solitary prayer and within a very short time God began to fall on Laughor. His family first felt the impact of the coming of the Spirit. Before long, great crowds were coming to Christ in overpowering numbers. All during this time, Roberts refused to let himself be photographed by any member of the press and he granted public interviews to no one. He knew he was nothing and he wanted to avoid the excesses of media arrogance. He had no desire to touch the world in his own name. Jesus was enough for Evan Roberts—and when Jesus is enough, men and women cry out as did Elijah of old: "How long halt ye between two opinions? If the LORD be God, follow him: but if Baal, then follow him . . . and the God who answereth by fire, let him be God" (1 Kings 18:21, 24, KJV).

We are slow to learn that we cannot kindle the fire we

crave. Yet we push forward, thinking, *If only we hurry a little more and buy more manuals and attend more conferences and take more notes, then surely then the fire will fall.* How plastic we become. We have but to look around us to see that our best piety is written on our T-shirts. No wonder we are unaccustomed to flame.

I wonder if, out there in the future, God isn't going to write Ichabod—"the glory of the LORD has departed"—across our neurotic strivings. Could it be he is praying for a new breed of men and women to bring hope to our plastic culture?

THE FIRE NEXT TIME

Recall the rhyme popularized by a great African-American spiritual:

> God gave Noah the rainbow sign.
> No more water, the fire next time.

Both testaments offer a high and heady sense of apocalypse. God always has been coming to the earth, his arrival imminent and thick with portent. God rides the clouds in thunder and lightning. His ride is heavy with judgment.

To some degree this imagery appends to the Holy Spirit of God. John the Baptist said as he began to baptize in Jordan, "I baptize with water, but there cometh one after me, the latchet of whose shoes I am not worthy to stoop down and unloose. He will baptize you with fire and with the Holy Spirit" (Luke 3:15, KJV). The Bible always attributes the energy of apocalypse to the fire of the Spirit. This fire would blaze across the continents of the unredeemed world and would leave a new order of things after its passing.

This same imagery appends to the Son of God. His final judgment comes in wrath and fire, a highly militant image. Julia Ward Howe wrote of it this way:

> Mine eyes have seen the glory of the coming of the Lord,
> He is trampling out the vintage where the grapes of wrath
> are stored,
> I have seen the fateful lightning of his terrible swift sword,
> His truth is marching on.

If this were not militant enough, another verse of the same poem emphasizes the fire of apocalypse even more:

> I have seen him in the watch-fires of a hundred circling
> camps,
> They have builded him an altar in the evening dews and
> damps . . .

As the end draws near, God will measure the world by harsh standards and answer all with fire.

So the tongues of flame that appear over the disciple's heads on the Day of Pentecost symbolize God's reign, both militant and purging. The fire reminds us that all things are due for a final renovation at the coming of the Lord.

THE INDOMITABLE IMAGE OF PENTECOST

In my recent book *Miracles and Wonders* I told a story from my youth that bears repeating.

When I was a child, a bunch of us gathered about the Loomis house on a very windy day. Mr. Loomis was a huge man with a fearsome demeanor and we neighborhood children feared him greatly. He seemed the kind of man who would come upon us in the darkness, like a fiend from the fields of tombs. He made brooms and had huge knives that cut the hard straw (but which might just as easily cut up little Baptist and Pentecostal children).

And there, in his yard, we children began playing an interesting game with matches. We each took a match, lit it and threw it in the dry grass. We let the circle of fire grow until it reached a very large size, and then we worked at stamping it out. The winners never called for help and by themselves confidently stamped out the flame, which began to be driven by the wind. I determined I would win. I lit the grass on fire and let the circle of fire grow until it defied reason. Then I began to try to stamp it out. But the wind had stiffened to a gale and the fire began to spread. Suddenly I knew I could not possibly stamp it out.

I panicked and watched in horror as the growing circle of fire moved up to Mr. Loomis's house and began to travel up the corner and along the walls. My mother called the fire department; a great clanging and furor accompanied the arrival of several huge, red trucks. The whole community gathered to see my foolish arson. While the raging flames ate at his house, Mr. Loomis—the Boo Radley of my to-kill-a-mockingbird world— came out. I shrunk back in terror from this huge, white-bearded man who glared at me. My little friend, Frances, told me that while I had won the contest of who could build the biggest fire, I was sure to be put in prison for life and that they'd never let in my mother to see me.

On roared the flames.

I asked my mother if I would have to go to prison, and when she said, "I hope so," I broke into tears. The moment she saw how very heartbroken and how frightened I felt, she said that probably I would "go only to the county jail." But actually, I never had to go to either place, and I am still free of any enduring prison record.

While I never became a pyromaniac, I learned that day the overwhelming secret of fire: fire is driven by its hunger to devour. Fire is prone to break out of control. Fire upsets the community, filling it with fear and wonder.

Maybe that's why it remains the indomitable image of Pentecost.

3

THE OIL

Lord, today, by the mystery of Pentecost
you sanctify your Church among all peoples and nations.
Pour out the gifts of the Holy Spirit
over the whole world
and continue in the hearts of believers
that work of love which you began
at the first preaching of the Gospel.[1]

PRAYER FROM THE
EUCHARIST

One year following World War II, a refinery only a mile from my Oklahoma home burst into flame. I can still remember the orange fire against the black sky and I recall the sense of apocalypse that visited my childhood that day.

Oil is the food of the flame and it provides us with a potent symbol of God's warmth in an arctic world. No wonder Isaiah cried out about the glad oil of the anointing when he prophesied, "The Spirit of the Sovereign LORD is on me, because the LORD has anointed me" (Isa. 61:1, NIV). Such an anointing oil is the fluid symbol of God's presence.

GOD FLOWING FREELY

Oil is a tangible icon of God flowing freely through the world. In 1 Samuel, the old prophet goes twice to anoint David as king. I can only imagine that when he lifts the horn and pours the oil, an ordinary shepherd somehow gets changed into a monarch. Nothing of royalty is inherent in the oil. Yet as the oil, thick and heavy, rolls down David's head and face, the young shepherd feels its fluid witness and knows that the viscous, flowing substance is changing his destiny even as it flows. Oil has come to symbolize our own sanctification, our consecration, our certainty of God's presence in life.

We may be in danger of losing the force of this beautiful symbol of the Spirit. Indeed, we may already have lost it. Christians have more often selected the dove, which since pre-Renaissance times has occupied the poetry and literature of the church. The dove as the Spirit seems to have become the obsession of artists. When I first visited the Prado in Madrid, I felt struck by the majesty of an El Greco painting called *La Trinidad* (*The Trinity*). The painting shows God the Father as a godly old man, bearded and looking very much like a Spanish Inquisitor. The Father is receiving the wounded, naked body of Christ, the Son, from the tomb. Over the heads of both of them flutters a dove. This kind of representation of the

Trinity once was common. While it may be less so now, the dove still dominates as a symbol of the Spirit.

Yet it is odd that this should be so, for the Holy Spirit as a dove receives only one or two mentions in the Bible. The metaphor of oil appears far more often. In fact, Scripture mentions oil in one context or another some 193 times.

THE OIL OF HEALING

I attended a healing service recently at which a dynamic young pastor confessed to all of us that her life stood under judgment. She asked if we would anoint her with oil and pray for her healing. We examined the passage in James 5:14 as we gathered in a circle of prayer. Each of us took a small vial of oil and anointed this pastor and prayed for her healing.

The incident took place so recently in my life that I can give no report as to whether the woman has received her healing. But this was our prayer, and even as our small samples of oil spilled over her head and shoulders, we mingled our earnest prayers with that anointing. Who could deny the presence of the Holy Spirit in that room as the oil flowed? Suddenly I understood how very appropriate oil is as a symbol of the healing presence of the Spirit.

I somehow envy the new rite that Catholics have adopted for using oil to heal the sick. As the oil falls on the head of the suffering person, the minister says:

Lord God, loving Father,
You bring healing to the sick through your
Son, Jesus Christ.
Hear us as we pray to you in faith,

and send the Holy Spirit, man's Helper and Friend,
upon this oil, which nature has provided to
serve the needs of men.
May your blessing
come upon all who are anointed with this oil,
that they may be freed from pain and illness
and made well again in body, mind, and soul.
Father, may this oil be blessed for our use
in the name of our Lord Jesus Christ.[2]

How glorious that we can offer such an anointing of hope!

Oil was the number one prescription of apothecaries in the centuries that preceded modern medicine. They used it to heal, especially in combination with other herbs and minerals. But in a passage like James 5:14, healing flows as God inhabits the oil, consecrated by prayer. In this passage, oil—a universal and common home-remedy—takes on the power of the Almighty.

But oil is more than a primitive home remedy; it is a curative inhabited by God. When the Good Samaritan comes upon a poor, wounded soul beaten by brigands and robbers, he bandages his wounds, pouring on oil and wine (Luke 10:34). And then what? Healing, mysterious and wonderful, compassionate and certain, falls upon the man.

Health and holiness and the presence of God inhabit this beautiful symbol. Note the relationship between "holy" and "whole." In our sin and neediness we are not completely whole. We remain divided in our loyalties and our morality. We remain partial in our integrity, in our fairness and in our loyalties. We are Jekyll and Hyde creatures, all bundled into one miserable soul. We want what God wants—but we also want what we want. We bring our two-souled selves, well partitioned, into God's wholeness. In this divided state, loving both God and ourselves, we become captive to a hypocrisy of life in two modes, serving two different minds. Heaven does not welcome such a division. Neither should earth.

THE OIL OF DESIGNATION

Beginning in the book of Exodus, oil was used to designate sacred places or people. Whenever someone poured oil on either a person or a place, that person or place became somehow special in the plan and purpose of God. Jacob twice anoints altars at Bethel to designate them as special to God (Gen. 28:18, and 35:14). Where the oil fell, the altar became special to God.

As pastor of a growing church, I had the opportunity to baptize thousands of people (nearly 3,000). I reminded each new convert that when he or she came forward for baptism, most of the witnesses would not long remember their names, but would recognize them as people designated by the ritual to be in a new relationship with Christ. In a similar way, the oil we used to anoint the pastor designated her as belonging to God. The oil designated the arena in which we expect to see God work.

Always the presence of the Holy Spirit designates us as the property of God. This is true whether any oil is used to "seal the deal." The angel says to Mary in Luke 1:35, "The Holy Spirit will come upon you, and the power of the Most High will overshadow you. So the holy one to be born will be called the Son of God" (NIV). It is clear that God designates Mary as a vessel for his use. In Exodus 29:7, Moses anoints Aaron with oil, thus designating him as a special servant. Such anointings imply that the Holy Spirit will work through these designated people to perform the work of God.

I have a pentecostal missionary friend whom I have long admired. He always carries a bit of oil in his pocket. In hospital rooms and at other moments of human desperation he is prone to anoint—with their permission—all who can willingly see the oil as marking the special province of God. I have seen him do this so often, I have become convinced that oil is but a glistening witness that God is alive in the world and is marking out his territory for his own purposes.

When I first met my missionary friend, he was serving in Costa Rica. He lived in primitive settings, often walking among the sick and those in need of Christ. He would frequently pray for the uneducated villagers who saw his little flask of oil as a chalice of power. It seemed to these souls that they were touched with the vast possibilities of God—a grace they could never reckon for on their own. To be anointed was to be marked as the arena where *anything could happen*. The oil brought God near. It was enough. It was glorious.

THE OIL OF CONSECRATION

In Psalm 23:5, David, a grown man and a king of some years, still celebrates his consecration to the special task of God. As a professor in a seminary, many times I have been called upon to assist in the ordination of my students. I have ever been humbled by the act of consecrating these talented and committed young people for whatever use God has chosen for them. The best feelings come when I realize that I am not merely helping them enter a lifetime occupation such as banking or law; I am actually helping the church consecrate a person for God's particular use.

I have never anointed any of these young men and women with the oil of consecration, but in my own mind, I work hard to make sure that everyone present—the candidate, the family, and the body of Christ—sees the rite of ordination in just this way. I am in love with the notion that no real person of God works for a salary, but that all of them serve out of consecration to the work of ministry.

It has been more than 45 years since I was ordained. I have often wondered if there doesn't exist more than a casual correlation between my long life of service and the seriousness with which I took my consecration to ministry. I believe there may be; there must be! For even in those dark times of ministry (and they come to all ministers), I could never shake this driving concept. God had set my life apart for sacred service! That has kept me going in the hard times and will keep me going still.

A pastor friend once called me to help him sort through some heavy days of hurt. He felt ready to throw in the towel. But we knelt and prayed and rehearsed how we had "gotten the towel," and reminded ourselves what Jesus did with one towel that far away night in the upper room. Then we remembered that Jesus did not choose an easy life because he liked easy living. He understood that he must live his life with a purpose. He had not been consecrated to some holy understanding of his vocation. But Jesus, always one with the Father, knew that every moment, every action of his thirty-three year life, was consecrated to his Father's will. He would save man—and this required a viewpoint that neither allowed him to quit nor complain.

We have to remember that the word "Christ" comes from the Greek word *Krio*, which means to "anoint with oil." This is symbolic in the case of Christ, since he was the anointed one of God to bring redemption to humankind. Yet the metaphor holds if we pull it out of the Greek and put it in the Hebrew *Messias*, for it also means, "to anoint with oil." Christ is the anointed one of God and marked from the foundation of the world to redeem the planet. The very title he wears demonstrates his consecration to the Father's will.

Somehow, this same *krio* image must be ours.

THE OIL OF PRESENCE

All who are anointed share a sense of grand togetherness in the Kingdom. This idea finds its root in all that Jesus has to say about the coming of the Holy Spirit in the Gospel of John. The primary purpose of the Holy Spirit, Jesus says, is his accompaniment of all who believe in Jesus as the Christ. "I will ask the Father, and he will give you another Counselor to be with you forever" (John 14:16, NIV). The Holy Spirit is to be the symbol of God's unforsaking presence in our lives.

But the oil of anointing also signifies the Spirit's presence in our lives. The Psalmist writes:

I have found David my servant;
    with my sacred oil I have anointed him.
My hand will sustain him;
    surely my arm with strengthen him. . . .
I will maintain my love to him forever
(Ps. 89:20, 28A, NIV).

The oil of his anointing gives us the promise of his presence. Therefore the Holy Spirit's most wonderful ministry among us is just that: *He is among us!* He always will be. We have the enduring promise of his presence.

The most remarkable and most necessary of all the Spirit's gifts involves his presence. I have a friend who languished in a communist prison cell for four years during the early years of Cuba's Castro regime. He confessed to me that there never was a day of his suffering that he did not rely on the presence of the Holy Spirit to get him through his ordeal.

The ancients saw oil as a liquid of permanence. Streams of water dried up in seasons of drought and the land fell into a parched state when water disappeared in the high desert heat. But oil lingered throughout the long, arid seasons. Listen to Jesus' most significant promise on the day of his return to the Father: "Lo, I am with you always, even to the end of the age" (Mt. 28:20, NASB).

The stable liquid of oil does not dissipate nor disappear in the dry seasons of our lives. It is precious because it is so permanent. Oil symbolizes the continuing presence of the Holy Spirit.

THE OIL OF FILLING

The Bible often pictures the Spirit of God in the imagery of pouring or "filling." In Isaiah, God promises to pour out his Spirit on Israel's offspring (Isa. 44:3). In Ezekiel, God promises to pour out his Spirit on the house of Israel (Ezek. 39:27–29). In Joel (in the passage quoted by Peter in the Acts 2 sermon), God says he will pour out his Spirit on all flesh (Joel 2:28). This imagery from the temple suggests that God is pouring out his presence as a priest would empty a vial of oil in sacrifice.

In the New Testament, Paul declares his desire to be filled "to the measure of all the fullness of God" (Eph. 3:19, NIV). Paul craved "fullness in Christ" (Col. 2:10). As for all of those to whom Paul ministered, he prayed that they, too, would be filled "with the knowledge of his will through all spiritual wisdom and understanding" (Col. 1:9, NIV). The oil represents this pouring, this libation of God. Who would not treasure such an anointing?

The use of the word "fill" also dominates in the book of Acts.

The Holy Spirit at his coming "filled" all the house where the disciples sat, till they were all filled with the Holy Ghost (Acts 2:2, 4).

In Acts 3:10, the disciples are all filled with the Holy Spirit and with wonder.

In Acts 4:8, Peter is filled with the Holy Spirit, and later in the same chapter (Acts 4:31), all the people are filled with the Holy Spirit. Sometimes the apostles command that a people be filled with the Holy Spirit (Acts 9:17).

The metaphor of filling also dominates in Paul's letters:

Paul commands us all to be filled with joy (Rom. 15:13).

He says that God is eager to fill all things with himself (Eph 4:10).

He commands us to be filled with the Spirit (Eph. 5:18).

Why so much emphasis on being filled with the Spirit?

In life, nothing feels quite so derelict as the sensation of emptiness, the feeling that we have been drained of all reasonable resources. At such moments, we feel as though we cannot cope, because nothing of substance remains within. Our "emptiness" craves his filling. We despise this inner vacuum that leaves us naked before the slashing demons of our despair. We have no reply to the great questions of existence. Such feelings provide the fodder and straw that build a nest of suicide.

Every time I have felt this odd depletion, I have returned to only one answer. I crave a downpour of substance to fill the vacuum where my heart used to be. I believe that in such moments, God can supernaturally download his holy substance into my emptiness. His filling gives me that glorious sense of "life worth" once again.

I believe that a lack of the spiritual disciplines always triggers this periodic emptiness. That is, when I quit making myself pray, study the Scripture, and minister in his name, I become depleted. In fact, ministry alone may become an unimaginable drain on my inner sense of fullness. I often felt after Sunday morning services that a great many well-meaning people would come up to me to plug their umbilicals into my sparse inner resources and thus drain me dry. Sometimes these were sycophants who consistently stole whatever inner strength I had gained from my spiritual disciplines because they had none of their own. They refused to practice the disciplines and so always felt empty. All strength ultimately resides in the spiritual disciplines.

But why would I define the disciplines as "making myself" pray, study and minister? Because I believe that, in a large sense, that is how the disciplines work. Many do not yet see that while they are saved by grace, they grow by discipline. Grace cost God all he had, but it is absolutely free to us. Grace is therefore God's gift to us. Our gift to God is discipline.

God will never make us say a single prayer or read a single page of the Bible or minister to a single person in need. If ever we do these disciplinary things, we must do it out of our own desire to "make ourselves" do it, for if we lack this sense of putting the pressure on ourselves, we will likely not give God anything. Discipline rises from our own souls. It is a high gift that blesses us with inwardness, even as it pleases God that we willingly "make ourselves" do what is right even when we don't feel like it. Emptiness results from poor discipline.

To be filled with the Spirit we have but to ask. Yet we must ask with the eager desire to know his gracious substance. That is, we have to feel our emptiness and despise the state. We have to get sick and tired of being empty. Then, when we have faced the fatigue of our poor, vacuous souls, the Spirit comes to fill us.

THE OIL OF GLADNESS

Both Psalm 45:7 and Hebrews 1:9 speak of the oil of gladness. This fitting metaphor of the Spirit conjures up a kind of beatific, anointed face locked in laughter, with streaming oil pouring across a glad countenance. I particularly like the metaphor as it manifests itself in those few churches whose worship and lifestyle exudes spontaneity and joy.

I have come to esteem the *Book of Common Prayer* and all things Episcopal. Unfortunately, I came late to this esteem. The style and content of the book would not have interested me in the naïve, formative years of my faith. I seldom attended the more primitive church services of my youth but that I felt filled with joy. I know now that I can attribute the feeling largely to the company I kept. Somehow it seemed to me that they made experiencing joy the object of their worship. In other words, to some degree they went to church to "get happy." I realize now that this is not the best order of things. Happiness should be the result of meeting with God, not the goal of worship. Still, I must confess that in many a dour, bland worship service of those with more liturgical tastes, I have seen the shortcomings of those who pursue substance to a fault.

Most of us carry a great deal of pain into worship. Half of all those who enter any church on Sunday, do so while carrying some burden. They need a generous anointing with the oil of gladness. But alas, church carries them into no elevation of spirit. They come and go with their troubles. How sad! They cry out to be made lighter, but continue their weighty oppression. They receive no washing with the oil of gladness.

The oil of the Spirit would flow gladness into needy lives if we would but let him do it. Herbert F. Brokering wrote:

> To one who remembers the Spirit
> there is always a way out,
> even in the wilderness with the devil.[3]

The oil of gladness provides the way out of the debilitating slavery of depression.

I have a late friend who for years symbolized everything wonderful and light. Yet she had an odd discrepancy in her joy. For years she carried a huge burden for a renegade child. The boy had wasted his life in wild living and excess. She had wept her way across the years in an effort to restore him to productive living. He broke her heart again and again.

Yet, for all her brokenness, everything grew brighter the moment she walked into a room. She never forced her mood upon me, and yet her presence made me feel that no suffering could be legitimate in the presence of the Savior. She loved Christ—she would have said "Jesus"—and the ardor of her love distilled as sunshine. I loved hanging around her. I never heard her complain or gossip. Some people must have displeased her, but she never criticized them. Her entire life seemed baptized in the oil of gladness.

A flat, expressionless worship of God has never attracted a single soul to the faith. There is something both eruptive and disruptive about the oil of gladness. It is eruptive because, like Vesuvius, it always seems about to burst forth. It hides underneath all things hard to contain until it titillates our attachment. We feel that if only we stay a bit longer, it will burst forth and renew all those who stand near.

And it is disruptive, like a group of pre-adolescent children with the giggles in church who know they shouldn't have them, but alas, they do. They cannot contain themselves. And so for them the matrix of their dull little lives gets put to flight by an inner, happy force beyond their control. They know that even as they lose control they will be scolded or punished. Yet they have lost the power to stop giggling—something like what happens in Acts 2.

If the church is to find life, it must happen again to those who worship only the god of gray propriety.

WARMING THE UNBEARABLE CHILL

Oil is the Bible's metaphor of content and vitality. It's also the symbol of vitality and joy. Both items are often in short supply in the church.

I rarely worship where I can say that I experience a joy derived from God. Most of the joy I experience comes from clever planning and hype. I hunger for this transcendental joy that originates beyond the drab borders of human creativity.

Yet we can grow so dull to spiritual excellence that we feel content with mere human humdrum. This contentment reveals our depravity.

> Inside or outside the church, it is the people who are most concerned with finding God and with gaining religious truth who often have the most trouble with church. These twice-born people, who are congenitally sensitive to divine love, who seek it most sincerely and painfully, are the ones most hurt by the normal human fallibility and selfishness . . . the only persons who are truly comfortable with the church are those who have found some way of repressing, displacing, or denying their need for the experience of divine love.[4]

Those restless for more of God have found in the church too little of the oil of the Spirit.

The Holy Spirit does indeed long to transform these corpse-like churches until they are no longer lifeless and cold. The first step to return to life is to admit that what we have really isn't life, but a dull contentment with tasteless procedures that motivates none to hear our music or attend our sermons.

We are low on oil. The heat is off. The room is cold. We are empty and in need of God's filling. May it come to us soon! The dead must live. The chill is unbearable.

PART II

THE
MINISTRIES
OF THE
SPIRIT

৩৹

4

PRESENCE

By the Holy Spirit we are established as "friends of God,"
wherein that which is "specially proper to the friendship"
is "to take delight in a friend's presence," for "one reveals his
secrets to a friend by reason of their unity in affection, but the
same unity requires that what he has, he has in common with
the friend." [1]

THOMAS AQUINAS

Dorothy Sayers told of a Japanese Christian who admitted to some real confusion about the Trinity. The man felt baffled as any of us when we contemplate the mysteries of God's being. In struggling to understand the doctrine, he said, "Honorable Father, very good. Honorable Son, also very good. But honorable Bird, I do not understand at all." [2]

Certainly this Japanese Christian spoke for all of us who have ever stood dumbfounded before the majesty and awe of the Holy Spirit. Why is the Holy Spirit so difficult to understand? I like thinking of the Holy Spirit as the near side of the Trinity, but I must confess that despite his nearness, for most of us he remains more formidable to consider than the rest of the Trinity. The fact that he indwells me makes him no easier to understand.

I understand what the Father does in his creative role in the ordering of the cosmos and the universe. I understand what Jesus did in his redeeming work on the cross. But I am hard pressed to understand the exact nature of the Holy Spirit. Who is he? How does he come to me? When he does come, what does his coming mean?

THE EXOTIC PRESENCE

For all his mysterious involvement with us, the Spirit's elusive certainty feels exotic. The very warmth of his nearness leaves us enthralled before the almighty attributes of his presence. When Jesus talked about the coming of the Spirit, as reported in the book of John, he spoke of him almost entirely in terms of his presence. That presence is to be esteemed because of his power, vitality, and counsel. His presence endures forever. We are blessed to know that when Jesus said, "I will never leave you nor forsake you" (Heb. 13:5), the essence of this promise is kept by the unforsaking Spirit.

Jesus also spoke of the Spirit and his role in our spirituality: "If you love me, you will obey what I command. And I will ask the Father, and he will give you another Counselor to be with you forever—the Spirit of truth" (John 14:15–17, NIV).

Jesus promises that God will be with us in the form of a counselor. The Greek word *parakletos* means "counselor" or "one called alongside"—or more emphatically, "one called alongside *us*." Then he follows the promise with an even warmer word: "I will not leave you as orphans; I will come to you" (John 14:18, NIV).

Fifteen years ago our children enriched our lives through a foreign adoption. Suddenly we had a grandchild—and our joy knew no bounds. I remember going to the airport the night he arrived in the United States. After coming all the way from Calcutta by air, suddenly he entered our hearts and lives. His coming made us rich. But how much more is our grandchild made rich by the knowledge that he has parents? To be a child and to have a father is the greatest of blessings.

John 14:18 records a beautiful passage on the Fatherhood of God. We are adopted (according to Paul in Romans 8) into the family of God when we believe. At that time the Spirit of God becomes the evidence and seal of our adoption. We hear the pathos in this promise Jesus speaks in John. Without this adoption, we would indeed remain as orphans in the universe. No Father? How lamentable.

The passage reminds me of a little-known novelist, who pictured the grieving dead on the day of resurrection being met by a neurotic son, who cried to them, "I was mistaken, I have no Father. You have no father. We are all orphans in the universe." Without the Comforter, the Counselor, of John 14, this would be all too true. So we must cherish the promise of the Spirit: "I will not leave you as orphans." On the basis of this promise, we may celebrate our gracious entrance into the family of God and long all the more for our Father.

COMFORTER AND COUNSELOR

Jesus uses the terms Counselor and Comforter almost inter-changeably. Jesus understood that when he returned to heaven, we would long for a better and closer relationship with him. He knew that when he left us, we would remain behind in a kind of grief and bereavement over our loss. The disciples knew he was alive, for he had shown himself forty days after he rose from the grave and again lived among them. But now for ten days between his ascension and the coming of the Holy Spirit in Acts 2, Jesus had disappeared and they grieved his absence. So the Holy Spirit came at last to offer not just his presence, but to offer them an end to their grief and bereavement. For their beloved Jesus, in the person of the Holy Spirit, had come back to them in a completely different form.

What does this mean to us? The Holy Spirit is not just some ethereal theological concept; he is God, the near God. He is back among us, comforting all of us who wait with un-requited longing until we can see our Savior once again. As be-lievers, we understand that Jesus did not send the Holy Spirit just to give us presence, but that the presence would bring us comfort.

The presence that Jesus promised in the Holy Spirit would teach us. He would remind us constantly of Christ's admonitions—and he would do it all from the inside out. So we often call the Holy Spirit "teacher" because he isn't merely present *with* us, he is present *within* us to offer the same instruction that Jesus would offer to us were he still here in bodily form. He is the Christ at hand, the Christ of every age. He, the power that fueled the apostles, is also the power that fuels us.

A final passage in John speaks of the Holy Spirit as our guide. "I have much more to say to you, more than you can now bear. But when he, the Spirit of truth, comes, he will guide you into all truth" (John 16:12–13, NIV). What did Jesus mean here? Not only will he be present to teach and to correct and to establish us in righteousness, but, "He will guide you into all truth. He will not speak on his own . . . he will tell you what is yet to come. He will bring glory to me by taking from what is mine and making it known to you. All that belongs to the Father is mine. That is why I said the Spirit will . . . make it known to you" (vv. 13–15). In this wonderful passage Jesus reminds us that the Spirit will remain in the world to continue to lead people to believe in Jesus Christ and to instruct the church. And through it all, he will leave us with a sense of his presence.

GOD, THE NEAR

Not only do we want the Holy Spirit to remain near to us; we want him to be active in our life. Yet I suppose that all of us from time to time have felt abandoned by the presence of God.

It is important when we feel abandoned or alone, or when we feel that God is not keeping his promise to be with us forever (Hebrews 13:5), that we turn immediately back to God. Then we must pray the prayer that Ignatius once offered in a Roman prison just before lions devoured him:

> Father, make us more like Jesus. Help us bear difficulty, pain, disappointment, and sorrow . . . we look to the day when we will be completely like Christ, because we will see . . . My passions are crucified, there is no heat in my

flesh, and a stream flows murmuring inside me—deep down
in me saying, "Come to the Father."[3]

How glorious this image! God is indeed, through his
Spirit, an ever-present, murmuring stream, deep down inside
us. And that stream will never cease its flowing, nor its incessant beckoning us toward the Father.

But the nearness of God can be fearsome. A mother of a
naughty little girl instructed her to go up to bed. She told her
child to get down on her knees and confess to God that she had
been very naughty, and she reminded her daughter that God
was in her room and he would hear her. When the little girl
began her prayers, she said, "God, I want to tell you I've been
very naughty—but if you are right here in my room, God,
don't you say anything, 'cause it will scare me to death."

We are, I suppose, intimidated by a sense of fear in the
presence of God. If we can live comfortably near this great
power that runs the whole universe and yet remain chatty and
comfortable, we have probably misunderstood the awesome
difference between ourselves and God.

The Holy Spirit does a second thing as he comes near: he
illuminates the Second Person of the Trinity to the point of
fear. In other words, it is the Holy Spirit's job to make Jesus
very real to us. When Jesus becomes very real to us, we may actually feel ourselves a little afraid. I've never talked to anyone
who did not experience this sense of fear, almost to the extent
I've just described. When they have entered some moment of
closet prayer and seek to move in close to Christ, they suddenly
see his glory and tremble at his nearness. Because they hungered for his intimate presence, the Spirit brings Jesus Christ
thoroughly alive—and in the moment of his coming, they

tremble. They fear that if they should open their eyes, the reality of Christ had become so great around them they might actually see him and the terror of his imminent reality would destroy them.

Oh, that more people hungered for his nearness, to this extent! But for the most part, I suspect we feel far too comfortable with our mediocrity; our remoteness from God cannot threaten us. We lack the ability to hunger enough for God to draw ourselves into close proximity to Christ. I once wrote of my confidence in these four lines:

In search of God I often tear
My ordered universe apart.
To find that when my search is done
I found him in my very heart.[4]

The Apostle Paul tells us, "But we all, with unveiled face, beholding as in a mirror the glory of the Lord, are being transformed into the same image from glory to glory, just as by the Spirit of the Lord" (2 Cor. 3:18, NKJV). In other words, Paul says the Holy Spirit moves us ever further into a desire to experience full intimacy with Christ. And sweet this intimacy is! Oddly, this intimacy grows even sweeter when we enter a state of brokenness. Paul confessed to a "thorn in the flesh" that had left him feeling broken and defeated. On three occasions he had asked God to heal his inner pain. But God had not done so, telling Paul, "my strength is made perfect in weakness" (2 Cor. 12:9). Pain elicits the coming of the counselor. "The true Christian is like sandalwood, which imparts its fragrance to the axe which cuts it," said Sundar Singh.[5]

But is it possible that we might actually *fear* this intimacy? We fear the nearness of God because as God comes near, our obligation to live more as Jesus wants us to live becomes intensive. And this is wonderful. We should not fear this, for the intensity with which we hunger for the nearness of God acts like a magnetic force that draws us into the fullness of his presence.

God the Spirit has made himself accessible to us. He is the near side of the Trinity. He is our joy. He is our peace. We are to walk with him and love the stroll.

GOD, THE CONVICTING PRESENCE

One of the roles of the Holy Spirit is to convict us of our sin. As odd as it may sound, our misery over our sin really proves that we're Christians. In his wonderful book on grace and discipline (*Holiness by Grace*, 2001), Bryan Chappel says that unless we feel miserable after we sin, we have no right to claim that the Holy Spirit is in our lives at all. Christians possessed by the Holy Spirit should always feels a sense of conviction when they do wrong. No inner conviction, no proof we are filled with the presence of God.

Robert McQuilkin tells of a Japanese Christian who had trouble understanding what he should feel when his willfulness displaced his holiness in Christ. This man could not understand how he could move away from fellowship in Christ and still remain a Christian.

> Matsuyama slumped cross-legged on the wooden floor of his third-floor apartment. Apartment? It was one room for a family of four on the second floor of a former army bar-

racks. The ramshackled old building was now serving out its last days as housing for dozens of poor families.

"What's wrong, Matsuyama San?"

"I'm not a Christian any longer."

"What happened?"

"Oh, I got drunk, some guy bad-mouthed me, and I chased him with a baseball bat. What's worse, when I got home and told my wife, she handed me the butcher knife. She said, 'the Bible says if your right hand does wrong, cut it off.' I'm no Christian."

It was out of drunkenness that Matsuyama had been saved. An excellent electrician, he descended down the river of alcohol to poverty, taking his wife and three children with him. "Did you ever get drunk and fight before you became a Christian?" I asked.

"All the time."

"Did you feel bad about it?"

"Only if I got beat."

"Don't you see, Matsuyama San? Since the Holy Spirit lives in you, when you fail you're miserable. Your misery is proof you really *are* a Christian!"[6]

In a real sense, this is the devil's biggest ploy. If he can make us feel lost after we are saved, then we are bound to live a life of defeat. God certainly doesn't want this.

C.S. Lewis in *The Screwtape Letters* has Screwtape teach Wormwood that the best way to defeat young believers is to get them to believe that the wrong they have done is irreversible and unforgivable. If the devil can make us feel that we have no hope when we ask for forgiveness, then our forgiveness will seem impossible. We *should* feel miserable when we sin—but we must take our sin back to the cross and leave it there. Then we must count it as fact that God has forgiven us. If we cannot do this, our guilt will smother all sense of victory.

To choose to live for God is to choose to live in the light of his holiness. If we live in this bright light, we must not feel intimated by the shadows. I really do believe that this happens with all Christians who hunger for intimacy. I find it interesting that casual believers are generally "carnal Christians" who live a remorseless faith born out of their high level of tolerance with sin. They sin but rarely think about asking for forgiveness. On the surface, these Christians may appear to enjoy a very happy life. But in truth, not much goes on in their affair with Christ.

I said earlier that all who live in the bright light must not feel intimidated by shadows. I meant that the closer we live to light, the darker the shadows will fall. And when we live in the glaring light of the presence of Jesus Christ, we may expect the shadows to fall frequently and vividly around us.

GOD, KEEPING THE PRESENCE PRESENT

McQuilkin lists five steps to maintaining an ongoing companionship with Jesus Christ:

1. We must have a regular time to read and meditate on a passage of Scripture.
2. We must regularly worship God, giving him thanks for all he is.
3. We must pray not only for ourselves, but also for all the world around us.
4. We must regularly set aside time to meditate, study and pray.

5. We must practice the art of momentary confession of our sins, admitting and forsaking them the moment we transgress the expectation of God.[7]

Keeping the presence present demands that we find a balance in two things. We must always seek the inward life via the prayer closet where we move inward with Christ, even as we try to maintain an outward life in the world.

This is perhaps the hardest paradox that I know. We who love Jesus must seek his pleasure. Yet we must also intermittently leave the prayer closet, departing from our focus on adoring Christ as we begin to focus on the needs of the world around us. This has always been a conundrum of the church. The monks, if they have any glaring sin, may find their wrongdoing in shutting themselves away from the larger world, where hurt and pain and death run rampant. On the other hand, most ministers have an opposite problem. They become so relational in their ministerial style that they feel no need to enter the prayer closet. Oh, that monks and glad handers might blend their extremes into a middle way!

We need to pursue the balanced life. We must move freely between these poles: the intermittent monasticism of seeking Jesus Christ in the study, and venturing into the outer, needy world. This focus becomes the key to enjoying a victorious life: centering on Jesus in the closet and then focusing on the same Jesus as he leads us to serve in the outer world. We must never delude ourselves. Jesus lives in both places.

Perhaps one big temptation that blocks the way to both inwardness and ministry is the entertainment syndrome that sometimes characterizes the contemporary church. We may forget that the size of the crowd can turn our worship into a numbers game that bypasses real praise and only lauds our own success.

As Christians we must understand that the size of the crowd may become a great impetus to both ministry and the inner life. Certainly we feel a swelling sense of victory when a lot of people become lost in praise in one great worship service. But no church can become either big or great if it believes that Christians can serve only through worship. Great churches teach their people to lay down their hymnals and prayer books and move from the closet of prayer into the needy world beyond it. Great churches believe that the Holy Spirit is equally present in both the prayer closet and throughout the entire human predicament.

MEETING EVERY TRIAL WITH CONFIDENCE

The presence of the Holy Spirit lives in this great promise: "I will never leave you nor forsake you."

His nearness sponsors our very potential and our victory. It is as the apostle wrote: "Thanks be to God! He gives us the victory through our Lord Jesus Christ" (1 Cor. 15:57, NIV). We can meet every trial with confidence, for "In all these things we are more than conquerors through him who loved us" (Rom. 8:37, NIV). These scriptures teach us that we can never reach our potential until we live continually in his presence. Walking in God's presence is its own reward. Rachel Scott, a victim of the Columbine massacre, touched the whole nation when she wrote:

> I have lost all of my friends at school. Now that I've begun to "walk my talk," they make fun of me . . . I am not going

to apologize for speaking the name of Jesus. I will take it. If my friends have to become my enemies for me to be with my best friend, Jesus, then that's fine with me . . . I am not going to hide the light that God has put into me. If I have to sacrifice everything, I will.[8]

Rachel understood that the presence of Christ is all that matters. The Spirit is that presence.

5

TRIUMPH

I believe that unarmed truth and unconditional
love will have the final word in reality.
This is why right, temporarily defeated,
is stronger than evil triumphant.[1]

MARTIN LUTHER KING, JR.

"Winning isn't everything," runs a popular cliché, "it's the only thing." We all want to be winners. Yet this may be the oddest, most unreasonable of all needs, since every human contest ends with both a winner and a loser. The lingering fear of losing perhaps comes in second to the worst of our fears: *being* a loser!

The Holy Spirit helps me to defeat this "I'm-a-loser" fear in three ways. First, he guarantees me that he will stay with me through my losses. Why is this important? Because any loss where my strong defender accompanies me is a bearable loss. Second, the Spirit guarantees me that I will win the war, if not all the individual battles of my life. I can stand my temporal losses because he has set them against the light of my ultimate victory. Finally, the Spirit encourages me to a life of utter yieldedness to God. When I no longer feel wrapped up in my need to win—because already I have given myself away—the importance of my wins and losses loses its power over me.

THE AUTHOR OF PERSONAL TRIUMPH

The issue of triumph never lies in who I am but in whom I contain. My triumph therefore lies in my willingness to be filled with the Great Achiever, the Holy Spirit. Once he involves himself in my circumstances, the unthinkable becomes the customary.

I think of it this way: if it were possible for me to go into PacBell Stadium in San Francisco and for one shining moment to be filled with the athletic power of Barry Bonds, I might achieve some of his moments of glory. If this great home run king, who has become so popular in our day, could infill my life with all his expertise and prowess, my world and reputation might change. At such a moment I would become capable of doing wonderful, ESPN sorts of things. I could never have achieved these things while relying on my own stumblebum abilities.

It is always this way when the Spirit of God visits our lives. In other writings I have set Ian Thomas's wisdom in the light: If you could visualize the Holy Spirit infilling your life as you might put your hand in a glove, you would begin to get the picture. You might then say to that glove, "glove, pick up that pen," or "glove, pick up that pencil." Of course, the empty glove is powerless to obey you. If you command only the empty glove, it cannot obey you because it is not filled with the power of a living hand.[2] In such a way the Bible lures us into a life of continual triumph when it encourages us to "be filled with the Spirit." With the Spirit's power inside us, we can do things previously unimaginable.

I keep a roster of heroes who accomplished amazing things that the world shall never know about. Most of these outstanding men and women are missionaries who served the Lord in difficult and distant places. They fought against huge odds, often single-handedly. When their missionary tours ended and they had grown much older, these strategic giants—because of living for years for a Titan Christ—could not see their own true size. They never thought of themselves as remarkable. They served under the compulsion of so great a love that they changed their community or nation. Yet somehow they missed seeing their true significance.

Why did they remain blind to the size of their achievements? Because the Holy Spirit who filled them, supplied the power to challenge and change those morally flawed cultures once held captive to toxic worldviews. They saw nothing unusual in yielding their lives to the Spirit in order to call the power from beyond themselves. It seemed to them to be just good business to yield to him whose existence empowered their own. Thinking Christians always allow the hand of God to fill the obedient glove of their fragile and frightened lives.

In the chapel at Beeson Divinity School in Birmingham, Alabama, there stand some six busts of strategic martyrs. I often study them while I wait for our weekly service to begin.

I gaze upon Dietrich Bonhoeffer, one of those busts. He could not have known in his last weeks or months that the power that God was working through his life would speak to millions who would come after him. Each time I read *The Cost of Discipleship*, I feel amazed at what happens when a plain old glove, a "convicted German felon," is willing to be filled with the hand of God.

Another of those busts portrays Bill Wallace of China. Wallace served in China during the last, dark days of the Chinese Republic, when Mao Tse Tung put great pressure on the armies of Chiang Kai Chek, driving him from the mainland. The conquering regime left Dr. Wallace a prisoner of an atheistic and abusive government. There in a prison cell, this committed physician was martyred for Jesus Christ. Did Wallace see himself as a hero? I doubt it. He saw himself as the glove into which the hand of God had been inserted to do mighty things.

Another of those busts depicts Lottie Moon. I see her as a woman always unsure of herself in many ways, and yet she has become probably the Southern Baptists' best-known icon in the arena of world missions. Why? To herself it must have seemed she had done nothing so very remarkable. She simply agreed to be a glove, eager to invite the hand of God to achieve his mighty triumph through her life.

When the Spirit camps out in the surrendered center of our lives, we may do unimaginably brave or courageous things . . . and never notice. Suddenly we seem to be symbols of God's triumph and yet remain totally blind to our own importance.

Triumph achieved in any other name is not a valid triumph. We only diminish ourselves when we try to claim the triumph of God as our own.

Robertson McQuilkin talks about our more selfish state of Christian service. We are somehow like toddlers, ever immature in all we do. Toddlers, he says, have property laws, all stated in terms of themselves:

1. If I like it, it's mine.
2. If it's in my hand, it's mine.
3. If I can take it from you, it's mine.
4. If I had it a little while ago, it's mine.
5. If it's mine, it must never appear to be yours in any way.
6. If I'm doing or building something, all the pieces are mine.
7. If it looks just like mine, it's mine.
8. If I saw it first, it's mine.
9. If you are playing with something and you put it down, it automatically becomes mine.
10. If it's broken, it's yours. (No, the pieces are probably still mine.)[3]

Maturity will help children de-centralize their egos. Spiritual maturity will also teach us to "re-centralize" God in our souls, teaching us to cherish our empty-glove status, while we await our filling with a new kind of power. This is how it should be. In the process of maturity we come to treasure a spirit of self-denial by which we nudge our world in the direction of God. Still, we want to become the greatest servants of God and can take no pleasure in living defeated lives. We want to live in triumph and we know that the key to this triumph is the Holy Spirit of God.

PRAYER POWER

Can we arrive at this state of overcoming triumph merely by wrangling through the trials of our lives? The answer must be that we seek God and yield to him. This yieldedness will make of us a formidable force in the world.

Yieldedness can become such a fearsome thing that it flags the cause of God before the face of hell. The most ordinary Christians come to see that they can challenge the prince of this world in a mightier name than their own—the name of Christ! His name becomes their chief joy and fondest delight, for their preoccupation with Jesus eliminates their fears.

What a remarkable thing that people who might seem to us as weak, or out of touch may live perfectly in league with God the Holy Spirit. People who may seem disenfranchised may in reality become the picture of triumph. What makes it all happen? It is not just yieldedness; it is a praying yieldedness.

The most noble of prayers may be, "God, enable me." We are most healthy when we refuse to perform for some private corner of our audience. We inhabit an entertainment-driven world and we may feel tempted to play at life for the sake of applause. But there is a better ovation we may win—the applause of God. It's an enduring applause brought on by the simple law of the glove and the hand. And those who know the thrill of this calling, delight to feel the strong fingers of God moving in power within their own weak lives. Such saints consistently pray, "Father, I ask for no ovations. I seek only to be used. Use me not to astound people, but to bring them to a renovation of spirit."

I can name two reasons why I like to visit the city of Rome. One, as I've already mentioned, is to visit the catacombs of Saint Sebastian. An inscription in that catacomb seems to suggest that both Paul and Peter once hid there from Nero's patricians as they sought refuge from persecution. The other place in Rome I like to visit is the chapel of the Quo Vadis.

An old story tells how during the persecutions of Nero, the despised and hunted Christians came to the Apostle Peter to ask him to leave Rome. His peers didn't want Peter to die, as so many Christian leaders were doing (about 75,000 died in the four years of Nero's reign). These Roman Christians wanted the apostle to go on living to counsel and direct the church in those difficult times. Peter yielded to their pressure and agreed to leave the city, believing that once he moved safely outside Rome, the church might once again flourish.

But as he journeyed out of the city, he met Jesus entering it. Jesus said to Peter, "Where are you going?" Peter told Jesus he was leaving Rome so he might better serve the church. Peter then asked Jesus, "*Quo Vadis Domine*"—"Where are you going, Master?" The Savior replied, "I'm going back into Rome to die if you leave it." Peter broke into tears, turned around and became a martyr by inverted crucifixion. It is said that at the very place where he turned, the footprints of Christ became emblazoned in the paving stones. On that spot believers erected the little chapel of the Quo Vadis to celebrate Peter's surrender.

It is an odd thing, I suppose, to think that Peter may have had a greater triumph than he ever knew. To most, this odd triumph appeared to be utter loss. But the triumph of a Spirit-filled saint is like that. Surrender to the possibility of loss brings to us the kind of victory we may not be able to see at the moment of our surrender.

CARING ABOUT THE RIGHT THINGS

God never intended that his church become a gallery where we exhibit our saints. God has always desired his church to be a center for mobilization where people pick up the right equipment to advance the Kingdom in a hostile world. It ought to be the place where the defeated come in, strip themselves of their weakness, then dress themselves in the power of the Holy Spirit. For the church to become such a center of triumph, she must allow the Spirit to lead in at least four areas.

First, the church must allow the Spirit to start or to stop any program that it has going. We live in a day and age when the church has become a centrifuge of godly madness. When I pick up the bulletin in many churches I visit—and I visit a lot of them—I see everything from multi-teamed softball programs to skydiving-for-Jesus squadrons. How can any Christian consider all this and not want to ask, "How much of this really is sponsored or initiated by the Holy Spirit?" Once we have successfully answered that question, we must ask ourselves a further question: "Is this church really free to stop any of these, or would the cessation of any of them make those connected to that program so angry as to quit the church?"

No church remains free when it feels coerced to keep a program going simply because of public opinion or because that program fills the busy agenda of some important member, or even some staff member. The church, to become the armory of triumph where the Holy Spirit lives and moves, must be the church always free to start or stop any kind of program.

Second, the church can become an armory of triumph only when it remains free to try any form of Christ-centered adoration. I suppose we all have to admit that we live in a world filled with worship wars. Sometimes when I hear Christians fighting over what kind of worship they like or don't like, I ask myself, "Is this fight in any way related to the agenda of God?" And the answer is always no.

How odd that we have viewed the church as our entertainment center where we applaud our favorite kind of worship and "boo" the kind we dislike. God has no favorite kind of worship. God seeks only sincere hearts, and whether a person enjoys one kind of taste in sermons or music has nothing to do with how God feels. God, I suspect, can receive worship in any form in which it comes. The triumphant life issues from sincere adoration, never from a critical spirit. Our criticism of worship has nothing to do with God's taste—only our own war-like preferences.

The late D.T. Niles said that the gospel would never be accepted in Africa until the gospel could be "drummed and danced." It probably is true that the kind of worship the average Zulu tribesman enjoys would not work at all in the Cathedral of Saint John the Divine in New York. Are both of them legal and within their rights? Are both of them eligible to become anthems of triumph in such radically different circumstances? The answer is, of course, yes. The Holy Spirit seeks sincerity in adoration, not the particular preference of one pressure group forcing its tastes on another. So to remain free to become the armory of triumph, every church must be able to choose any form of Christ-centered adoration that is genuine and real to that congregation.

Third, for a church to become an armory of triumph, it must go beyond promoting tolerance to promoting acceptance. The Spirit thrives at the center of such communities. This has always been a hard question for the church. In fact, churches through the ages often have become little enclaves of fighting and quarreling and struggling over race and differences in religion. It always amazes me how the Jews and the Samaritans fought all the way through the Bible—yet amazing or not, it seems customary.

All across America I've seen nativity sets done with African-American figures. And as I examine them I say to myself, "Isn't this as reasonable as having white, Nordic Europeans, rather like myself?" Yet I was well on my way to manhood before I stopped to consider that most of those who gathered around the original cradle likely were Semites. In fact, these figures probably looked more like Iraqis than my own race might. Once we understand and accept this, we English and Northern European Americans might find reason to shed our arrogance. If anyone has miscast the nativity of Christ, it is probably us. In these African-American nativities I see some other group taking a huge step of racial identity with Jesus. The Holy Spirit fosters all such identity, which must in the end be wholesome for all who take pleasure in allowing the world to seek Christ-likeness.

One of the great things to be said of Charles Finney, the nineteenth century evangelist, is that he never got so busy preaching Christ that he found it impossible to take strong stands against slavery. Finney's views, of course, earned him strong censure in some sections of America in when he preached. Yet he never varied from this one big notion, that all people were created in the image of God. He did not preach that we ought to tolerate each other; he preached acceptance. The Holy Spirit blessed Finney for his endorsement of racial equality. The armory of triumph will always move with those who preach acceptance. And I believe that sooner or later the God of all truth will honor all those who preach and teach accept-ance.

Fourth, the church can become an armory of triumph when it believes that God loves every individual the same. To try to understand this is to try to admit that when we go to war with other countries, we may not necessarily be expressing how God feels about the people of that land.

I think one of the most majestic moments in any contem-porary novel occurs in *All Quiet on the Western Front* when a German soldier and a French soldier fall into the same foxhole. As these two enemies lie there in the same foxhole, wounded and dying, they look at each other with a new kind of reserva-tion, a new kind of openness that says, "We really aren't that different after all." And then these sworn enemies, who only moments before had tried to kill each other, found out in their dying moments how much they were alike. They each took out their wallets to show the other pictures of their family, living on far separate continents. Not only do these enemies exhibit the same kind of basic needs and loves, they die cherishing the same values.

To enjoy personal triumph we must understand that the Holy Spirit blesses those who really can look upon their foes and think of all the similarities between them.

THE SOVEREIGNTY OF GOD OVER SIN

Personal triumph always involves seeing how we spend our love for God. God remains in charge of our lives no matter what circumstances surround us. When we come to Jesus Christ, we come with the understanding that this world can-not manipulate us in any unmerciful or final sense. In fact, triumph remains the name of the game. Paul would say it this way:

> As it is written: "For your sake we face death all day long; We are considered as sheep to be slaughtered." No, in all these things we are more than conquerors through him who loved us. For I am convinced that neither death nor life, neither angels nor demons, neither the present nor the future, nor any powers, neither height nor depth, nor anything else in all creation, will be able to separate us from the love of God that is in Christ Jesus our Lord (Rom. 8:36–39, NIV).

This means that we must never allow ourselves to languish under the circumstances of our lives, no matter how dehumanizing or complex they seem to be.

Many years ago Jack Taylor ran into an old friend whom he found moping along the sidewalk. This Christian friend seemed to be discouraged to the point of feeling completely out of victory. Jack spoke to him with all the cheer he could muster in an attempt to revive the dejected man's spirits.

"How are you doing?"

"I'm OK," his friend replied, "under the circumstances."

"What are you, as a Christian, doing *under* the circumstances?" Jack asked.

It was a fair question. Christians who believe in the message of Romans 8 have no business living under circumstance. God has placed all things beneath the feet of Christ.

> And what is the exceeding greatness of his power toward us who believe, according to the working of his mighty power, which he wrought in Christ, when he raised him from the

dead, and set him at his own right hand in the heavenly places, far above all principality, and power, and might, and dominion, and every name that is named, not only in this world, but also in that which is to come: And hath put all things under his feet, and gave him to be the head over all things (Eph. 1:19–22, KJV).

If all things remain under his feet, then surely the defeatist ups and downs of our lives live there, too. This being so, we sin against God's loving defeat of all our trials when we go on allowing them to control our lives or even our moods.

McQuilkin describes four priorities that will allow us to live on top of our circumstances. First, he says, we must be honest about whether we really want to be rid of our sins. Second, we must genuinely want to win our spiritual battles and remain willing to ask the Holy Spirit to guide us to a strategy of triumph. Third, we must choose the temptation we focus on so we don't take on an overwhelming assault all at once. Finally, we must carefully select strategies that we think will work for us.[4] If we do these things, we shall no doubt live and achieve, plotting our lives carefully in ways we know we can win. This is how the Spirit of God gives us life as we struggle to move on.

LIVING AND WINNING IN CHRIST

With all things under the feet of Christ, our future remains bright. We can live and win. That's wonderful, because our calling in Jesus Christ is living and winning.

I consider David Wilkerson to be one of the great Christians of the '70s and '80s. His New York ministry among drug-related gangs inspired a whole nation to believe that Jesus Christ had astonishing powers. While most psychologists insisted a bad drug habit could not be beaten and amounted to a slow death sentence, Wilkerson claimed that if he could get someone to experience the "fullness of the Spirit," that person could live free of his or her addiction.

The claim enraged many secular psychiatrists and even some church people. A part of their anger rose over the fact that Wilkerson at one time implied that a person had to speak in tongues to guarantee the Spirit's cure for hard-core addiction. I would not go so far as to say that "tongues" is an essential evidence of the Spirit's indwelling. But even if it were, it would seem a small trade for freedom from this monstrous killer.

Wilkerson was on the right track. The power of the Spirit is formidable. The filling of the Holy Spirit must indeed release in us the power to get free of all of Satan's abuses. To be filled with the Spirit is to release in us extraordinary powers, and if we yield to those powers, we shall indeed become people with lives marked by triumph. God, as it has been said, "don't sponsor no junk." When we are filled with the Holy Spirit of God and grant him full reign in our lives, we can never become the repositories of secular junk or half-cooked ideas or trashy philosophies. Rather, we shall live in the center of God's will and his triumph will become customary.

ILLUMINATION
OF THE WORD
MADE PRINT

The Bible has been called, with pardonable exaggeration,
"The Book of the Spirit."[1]

H. WHEELER ROBINSON

Todd Beamer has become a hero and martyr to Americans, an icon who earned our esteem without ever applying for it. Lisa Beamer, his widow, commented in her wonderful account of their marriage that one verse describes his heroism: "Greater love has no one than this, that one lay down his life for his friends" (John 15:13, NIV).[2]

We have all seen Todd's heroism and cannot but thank God for his self-sacrifice. Every time I see the capitol building on the evening news, I ask myself, "Would it still be there except for Todd Beamer?" Every American owes him at least our esteem.

But where did Todd's favorite Scripture come from? Jesus originally spoke these words before he went to the cross, as recorded in the Gospel of John—but where did the Gospel of John come from? From a fisherman? Just a fisherman? Or did it have a wider, deeper origin in God?

The Apostle Peter wrote long ago: "Above all, you must understand that no prophecy of Scripture came about by the prophet's own interpretation. For prophecy never had its origin in the will of man, but men spoke from God as they were carried along by the Holy Spirit" (2 Peter 1:20–21, NIV).

The Holy Spirit, then, inspired the phrase in John that so wonderfully describes Todd Beamer's sacrifice. But how does the Holy Spirit do this? The Spirit inspires and interprets Scripture. He moved in the life of John to record the words that described Christ's heroic act. And he speaks in our lives to inspire us as we read those same words.

SPEAKING THROUGH A TIME WARP

The Spirit speaks from ancient writers to modern readers through a kind of time warp. He spoke to John in the first century to write the words that describe Todd Beamer. And he speaks to us on the other end of the time-and-distance continuum in the twenty-first century as we read what he inspired John to write. God speaks through a synapse of centuries to inspire us on both ends of time.

A friend of mine recently suffered a heart attack while on a hunting trip. He survived in a miraculous way. Following his quintuple by-pass surgery, he came to cherish Psalm 116. The Holy Spirit applied these words directly to his heart.

> I love the LORD, for he heard my voice; he heard my cry
>   for mercy.
> Because he turned his ear to me,
> I will call on him as long as I live.
> The cords of death entangled me,
> the anguish of the grave came upon me;
>   I was overcome by trouble and sorrow.
> Then I called on the name of the LORD:
> "O LORD, save me!" . . .
> For you, O LORD, have delivered my soul from death,
> my eyes from tears,
> my feet from stumbling,
> that I may walk before the LORD
> in the land of the living
> (Psalm 116: 1-4; 8-9, NIV).

The Holy Spirit moved in centuries 2500 years apart when he caused the poet to write this Psalm and my stricken friend to cherish the words. The Spirit uses this wonderful "time warp" inspiration to create and use Scripture in widely separate centuries.

The Word of God is alive and powerful, piercing and discerning. You'll find those words in Hebrews 4:12, significant words that point us to Scripture to find the key to personal power and success in life, no matter our difficulties. But then, the Holy Spirit performs a role consistent with what he inspired the writer to record in Hebrews 4:12. This passage likens the

Bible to a *machaira*, a double-edged sword—a particularly significant word for sword.

The Roman infantry used the *machaira* as its main battle sword. It was not a long, imposing weapon. In fact, it was a very short sword whose double-edged blade extended out only about 18 inches. The enemies of Rome must have felt amused when they first saw these world conquerors and empire builders advancing into battle with such miniaturized weapons. But they changed their minds quickly once they saw how effectively the sword served in battle. Rome's legionaries could chop up all their opponents at close range. The Romans carved an empire out of a barbaric world with an eighteen-inch blade.

In a similar way, the sword of God's Word is our *machaira*, God's answer to life's smothering entanglements. The Bible is our best weapon of advance when the world closes in on us.

The Bible is the Holy Spirit's communiqué enabling God to keep an ongoing conversation with the world he loves. "All Scripture is God breathed," reads 2 Timothy 3:16, NIV. But what does this term "God-breathed" mean?

I well remember the first of the *Star Wars* trilogy, which instantly captivated many of us with the sinister breathing of villain Darth Vader. I can still see this fiendish giant, dressed in black and breathing like a demon with emphysema. The chill of his breath somehow sent a shiver through moviegoers.

In a far more positive way, it seems to me that when I hold the Scriptures to my ear—in very quiet moments when I most sense my need for God—I can hear the Holy Spirit breathing. And when I begin to read, his breath issues as confidence in my life. God's Word is God-breathed—as real as his respiration in our lives.

How and Why This Book Came to Be

The Bible is the Word of God, born of the Holy Spirit. But how did we get it? How did the Holy Spirit get it done?

The Spirit fell full force upon holy men and women and the words that flowed from their pens as they touched ink and paper. When he breathed upon that script, our calling to a meaningful destiny was born. This print became a "blue print" to our future.

But *how* did it come to us? Some religions teach that their sacred writings got handed down from the sky in some antiseptic, supernatural way. God, it seems, wrote specially to them in golden fire on tablets of platinum. Thus came the divine word, directly from heaven to earth, without ever passing through human trial or experience.

Not so the Bible. In writing the Bible, God seemed to consider human worth as altogether important. In writing the Bible, God determined that the human authors should not remain passive, mindless creatures. When the Spirit moved, the writers—with all their idiosyncrasies—listened, and the force of their humanity marked their writing. Should we not love the Great Holy Spirit because he considered human beings to be such key players in what God wanted to say?

Remember Peter's insistence that the Bible came into existence as holy men of old wrote (2 Pet. 1:21). God's Word was born in the lives of people—busy people, sinful people, needy people—and all their busyness, sin, and need readily show through. Thus the Word has a very human ring to it. The Bible is for people and through people, and the people who wrote it became so much a part of it that their individual writing styles came through. Ordinary "biblical" people made themselves available to God to speak his revelation to other ordinary, "contemporary" people like us. He spoke an honest Word, a perfect Word—a Word infallible.

The early Clark Pinnock wrote, "The chaos of American theology today can be traced back to its roots in the rejection of biblical infallibility . . . To move from the pages of scripture is to enter into the wastelands of our own subjectivity . . . The Bible is a divinely provided map of spiritual order. It contains the directions and markings to guide a person into reconciliation with God."[3]

But can the Holy Spirit really declare himself so infallibly through human beings in such a completely natural way? Wouldn't we have felt more impressed had he actually handed it down to us on golden plates, etched in letters of fire? It is pointless to discuss the matter. When the Spirit spoke, he used a most ordinary way of expressing himself. He chose the ABCs—or their Hebrew equivalent, *Aleph*, *Beth*, *Gimel*—to make himself known. He came in common nouns and verbs, in prepositions; the customary words that tumbled out of heaven through a thousand "thus sayeth the LORD's." While we feel mystified by their mysterious origins, we remain all the more certain of our own. God speaks, his messengers write, and we come to know who we are.

Years ago I found myself floundering in a huge identity crisis. I was attempting to plant a church and things hadn't gone well. A faithful Christian friend pointed out to me the word in Jeremiah: "For I know the thoughts that I think toward you, says the LORD, thoughts of peace and not of evil, to give you a future and a hope" (Jer. 29:11, NKJV). Suddenly the Spirit who urged Jeremiah to write had spoken to me as well, and I came to know who I was.

IS GOD'S WORD RELIABLE?

Can we count on the Word of God to tell the truth, the whole truth and nothing but the truth?

We who live in this day are not so very different from those who have lived in every other day. From century to century, the best of us all want the same thing. We want God. His Word assures us that we shall have him.

We can have all of God that we want. We crave him at the first light of morning and seek the warmth of his presence at chilling midnights. We want his ancient light that brightened those who knew him in dim yesterdays to shine on today's complexities. We want his unforsaking manna to fall in the deserts of our spiritual need. And we want the comfort of his book. It will always be there, always instructing us. "The grass withers and the flowers fall, but the word of our God stands forever" (Isa. 40:8, NIV).

But when we say that the Holy Spirit has inspired the Scripture, what do we mean? We mean that his Word is trustworthy. In recent times this has become a topic of frequent discussion. Is the Bible authoritative? Is it an incontrovertible truth? Scholars have bandied this issue around from seminary to seminary and from liberal pole to conservative viewpoint. What have they decided? Only this: the Bible is the Word of God and may be trusted to speak the truth to all who believe it.

But what about those who don't believe it? The Holy Spirit works generally in the lives of people of faith. The Bible was written by the Spirit through people of faith, to be read by people of faith. Without this, the Spirit's revealing work across the ages cannot be received. A Russian dictionary produced during the communist/atheistic era of that state contains this definition of God's Word: "a collection of fantastic legends without scientific support. It is full of dark hints, historical mistakes, and contradictions. It serves as a factor for gaining power and subjugating unknowing nations."[4]

On the contrary, the word for this Word most often used by evangelicals is *inerrant*. No mistakes! Some scholars want to define this term narrowly and some want to define it broadly, but the bulk of evangelicals believe that the Bible contains no falsehood in any part. Evangelicals are taught to have confidence in Scripture because it can be depended upon in every verse to tell us the truth. Evangelicals generally fear that if the Scripture lies in any part, it might lie in every part.

Henrietta Mears said that on one Sunday, Dr. Louis Evans, pastor of the Hollywood Presbyterian Church, was making just this point while preaching on the virgin birth of Christ.

> As he stood there in the pulpit, he said, "So if you don't believe the Virgin Birth, tear it out." With that statement he literally tore the pages out of his Bible and threw the pages over the pulpit. "If you don't believe he raised Lazarus from the dead, then tear that out." So he literally tore it out and threw it over the pulpit. "If you don't believe in the resurrection, then tear it out."
>
> And he literally tore the pages out and crumpled them and threw them over the pulpit. With those tattering pages floating down the pulpit, he said, "What do you have left? All you have left is the Sermon on the Mount, and it's not worth anything unless a divine Christ preached it." And with that he said, "Let's bow for the benediction."

As soon as he bowed his head, in that sedate, vast congregation, a man stood up and said, "No! No! We want more! More!" Then another fellow said, "Yeah, we want more!" So Evans picked up another Bible and preached for another fifty minutes. And then gave the benediction.[5]

Many translations throng our lives and the sheer number of them beg the question, "How can we be sure which Bible translation is the truest? Which is the most reliable? After all, the Word of God is being translated by so many different groups."

Never let the myriad versions suffocate you. You may be sure of this: nearly all Bible translators have a concern for honest scholarship and a high allegiance to the Holy Spirit whom they trust to lead them into truth.

THE INDWELLING WORD IN THE CRISES OF LIFE

I have passed many crises in my life and always in any predicament, I have clung to two things: the indwelling Holy Spirit of God and the Holy Bible, the book he wrote. The indwelling Spirit served as my "inner" witness while the Bible functioned as the time-honored "outer" witness I could hold in my hand.

At times, when my future felt neither under threat nor unclear, I trusted the Spirit and searched through the Word of God. Once, when my dearest friend died, the Spirit directed me to the Bible, which directed me to trust Christ in the crisis. The Bible has always furnished me with wings of hope to soar above the swamps of my despair. At those needy times I never picked up a Bible and thought, *what a neat translation!* Nor did I, while bleeding and hungering for a clear word from God, ever think of checking to see what other translations might say.

In my moments of real need, the issue of translations became a cold, frigid, theological distraction void of comfort.

Remember that the Spirit has for his greatest work the drawing of men and women into Christ. Anytime you start reading the Bible you may be sure that the Spirit will be there to illumine and apply the text to your need. No wonder Billy Sunday wrote:

Twenty-nine years ago, with the Holy Spirit as my Guide, I entered at the portico of Genesis, walked down the corridor as if the Old Testament are galleries, where pictures of Noah, Abraham, Moses, Joseph, Isaac, Jacob and Daniel hung on the walls. I passed into the music room of the Psalms, where the Spirit swept the keyboard of nature until it seemed every reed and pipe in God's great organ responds to the harp of David, the sweet singer of Israel.

I entered in to the chamber of Ecclesiastes, where the voice of the preacher is heard, and into the conservatory of Sharon and the lily of the valley where sweet spices filled and perfumed my life.

I entered into the business office of Proverbs and on into the observatory of the prophets where I saw telescopes of various sizes pointing to far off events, concentrating on the bright and morning Star, which was to rise above the moonlit hills of Judea for our salvation and redemption.

I entered the audience room of the King of kings, catching a vision written by Matthew, Mark, Luke and John. Thence into the correspondence room with Paul, Peter, James and John writing their Epistles.

I stopped into the throne room of Revelation, where tower the glittering peaks, where sits the King of kings upon his throne of glory with the healing of the nations in his hand, and I cried out:

All hail the power of Jesus' name,
Let angels prostrate fall;
Bring forth the Royal diadem
And crown him lord of all.[6]

The Bible is the Holy Spirit's great glass, given to us to summon the adoration that belongs to Jesus alone.

Remember, the main purpose of this book is to let the indwelling Spirit call us to Scripture to learn all we need to survive. But merely knowing all about the Book cannot sustain us. Only loving it will cause us to trust it, and trusting it will enable us to live victoriously. So come. Let us turn to the Spirit to make Christ real to us. Let us trust God's great book.

It is the sop against the teary face of our tragedies.

It is the tourniquet against the wound that kills.

It is a clear violin that roars above the cannonade.

It is a touch that tells us we are not alone.

It is the compass whose needle is set toward the throne.

It is the pole star whose wisdom is fixed and immovable in every crisis.

It is the holy Word, free of error, free of fraud,
Breathed by the holy breathing of our ever holy God
To make of us such creatures as angels might applaud.

How blessed odd that our Holy God, could give such needy sod

His healing, saving light—The Word, the Life, the Book of God.

THE ROLE OF THE HOLY SPIRIT IN REVEALING GOD'S WORD

As a boy I loved to play "hide-and-seek." The game requires that the players act somewhat deceptively. I always found the game as exhilarating as it was deceptive, however. I felt real agony in trying to find a hiding place so well concealed that my playmates would never guess it. I loved the grand moments of revelation. When their despair reached its zenith, I would jump out from behind a tree and cry, "Here I am!"

God plays no such deceptive games with us. He may sometimes hide himself from us (see Isa. 45:15), but for the most part, he longs to disclose himself to us. He has found a wonderful way to cry, "Here I am!" In the Bible he has done just that. In the fullness of his grace, he has decided to tell us who he is and what he is like. The Bible is God's great cry, "Here I am!" And the Holy Spirit lives inside us to point to him and say, "See, this is God, the God who loves you."

On a Sunday afternoon in September of 2001, Lisa Beamer visited the crash sight where Flight 93 ended (and where her husband's life ended as well). She confesses that she felt her stomach churning as she passed the road from Shanksville, where many stood to salute her bus as she passed. So many things raced through her mind. But as traumatic as it seemed, God declared himself. On a sunny, late summer day, with the temperature close to 70 degrees, Lisa gazed out over the crash site one final time. She saw a hawk circling above the field where her husband's plane had crashed. But she did not feel devastated. She wrote that a sense of peace possessed her and she remembered Isaiah 40:30-31:

Even the youths grow tired and weary,
and young men stumble and fall;
but those who hope in the Lord
will renew their strength.
they will soar on wings like eagles;
they will run and not grow weary,
they will walk and not faint.[7]

Lisa Beamer discovered that the Holy Spirit is like a flashlight given to us to shine into the dark, mystic fissure of this ancient Word. She also learned that God can declare himself even in the midst of the most titanic tragedies. Then we see God, for the Spirit loves to reveal him to us.

Every pagan temple gives evidence of a fierce yearning in the human heart to know God. But we spoil this game of religious Hide-and-Seek when we seek to pry God from his hiding place. He is best found in the document whose first line reads: "In the beginning." After all, that's as far back as we can go! And there, in clearly understandable words, the Holy Spirit reveals to us the hiding God who says in his Book, "I love you too much to remain hidden any longer. Seek me with all your heart in this book, for here I declare myself."

The word "revelation" means to bring something out of hiding. The word comes directly from the Greek New Testament as the word "apocalypse." The central idea of the term has to do with the drawing of drapes. In the theater, an apocalypse "throws back the curtains" and at once declares the hidden contents on stage.

My wife and I love theater. A good part of this love stems from that first moment when the curtains open. It's the same in any play we've ever seen. We fidget in our seats, waiting for the downbeat of the orchestra. We busy our minds, wondering what is already in place that will thrill our senses once the curtain parts and a new world opens to us. Could we ever grow tired of that magic moment of overture? The cymbals clash, the tympani rolls, the sluggish, abominable curtains creep apart . . . and a story is born.

In our hunger to know God, we never go to the theater alone. We are on a dramatic outing with the Holy Spirit. He is the producer of the apocalypse. He orders the curtains up and he sits with us throughout the play, helping us to interpret and to apply and to know what this great redemption drama really means, line by line.

THE SPIRIT AND THE WORD

The Bible is God's special manual of instruction.

I read the Bible in its original languages ever so slowly, lexicon in hand. I am not good enough at this to be a *real* Bible translator. My knowledge of Greek and Hebrew is in place, but inadequate. Still, recently I was selected to serve as a stylist on a translation team. Why? Not because I know the ancient languages well, but because they felt I knew English fairly well.

I have enjoyed my time on this team because of the thrill of working with a group of scholars at the task of translation. And what was my part? At best, I merely offered my counsel on how to make each translated sentence as readable and riveting as it might be.

As I worked on this Bible, I discovered myself getting to know the Holy Spirit fairly well. In fact, for the past three years that I have labored on this translation, I have lived very close to the words of a new, emerging English Bible. I have prayed over each of those words. I have asked the Holy Spirit to help me be as honest as possible that I might give the Hebrew and Greek texts their best chance to enjoy a good English life. I have baptized every word in the holy sweat of my intention. This has not been light work for me. I have spent my soul at this business. Ah, but the closeness I have discovered in relying on the Spirit has more than compensated me for all my fatigue!

In working as a part of this team I have chiseled each word of the Word of God from my very bones. I have agonized in my utter concern for my English readers. Yet never once did I try to call attention to the words I helped select. I agree with Andrew Wyeth, who said that our craft should never be exhibitionist. Rather, "the craft should be submerged . . . rightfully the handmaiden of beauty, power and emotional content."[8]

But "pretty" is not all it takes to make a translation. Integrity and ancient word meanings must ever remain in place. To accomplish this integrity, I found great joy in working with those "doctors" in the temple, who really do know and love the ancient manuscripts. But of greatest profit to me was to live at the command of the Spirit. My affair with him remained both exotic and inward.

THE GRAND SIMPLICITIES OF SCRIPTURE

I learned one further lesson from the Spirit. He glories in the simple word. He is not a God who delights in confusing us with deep, obscure words, once crafted in forgotten, ancient worlds. No, he wants us to understand as clearly as if we were reading today's newspaper.

When in 1517 Luther nailed his 95 theses to the church door, he left behind a particularly famous thesis: *Sola Scriptura*.

The words mean, "only the Scriptures." While the church argued for tradition to help determine the church's practice, Luther had come to believe that only what the Bible said should guide Christian living.

In subsequent years Luther determined to get the Bible out of Latin and into German. Why? Because few in his parish spoke Latin. He could read the ancient words, but he knew that was too narrow a market for something as wonderful as the Word of God. The Latin Word made sense to those who once spoke Latin, but by Luther's time, no one except the priests spoke it. The Word of God is for the common person. Luther understood this.

In many ways we might call the fifteenth century the Century of the Holy Spirit. Around Luther's time the world came alive with Bible translations. The Spirit himself began to live out a divine romance as the Bible swept in fury across an ignorant world, a planet astounded by the upfront simplicity of God's redemption story. During those years eight major English translations and revisions appeared. The Holy Spirit moved powerfully to make the Bible the property of all and not merely the Latin fascination of a few.

The Holy Spirit filled the lives of people like William Tyndale, who, like Luther, began to develop a concern that the Latin Bible held no answers for a people who couldn't read it. Tyndale had developed a real concern for the common person—the English plowboy, for instance, whom he said should be able to read the Bible at his plowing if he so desired. Erasmus, at Oxford, believed the same thing and wrote in his introduction to the New Testament: "Christ wishes his mysteries to be published as widely as possible. I could wish even all women to read the Gospels . . . that they might be read and known, not merely to the Scotch and the Irish, but even by Turks and Saracens. I wish that the husbandman might sing parts of them at his plow. That the weaver might warble them at his shuttle. That the traveler, with their narratives might beguile the weariness of the way."

When the King James Bible first appeared in 1611, only 3 million people in the world spoke English; but in the next four hundred years, that Bible helped to establish English as the *lingua franca* of the world. At the heart of Western culture has lingered the Spirit of God, stuck on one grand simplicity.

PREACHING TO HANSIE AND BETSY

Someone once asked Martin Luther if he felt insecure in preaching each week to the great Bible scholars that thronged his congregation. He smiled and confessed his secret for surviving in a world of eggheads. "When I preach," he confessed, "I preach to Hansie and Betsy. If they understand, so will the theologians present."[9]

Who is Hansie? Who is Betsy? They were German house maids who came to Luther's church with the same spiritual need as the theologians. But more than that, Hansie and Betsy are us. We, like them, rise early and work hard. Like Richard Cory, "we work and work and wait for light. We go without the meat and curse the bread."

Life has never been easy for Hansie and Betsy. They suffered with sickness and death. They dealt with job loss, desperation, depression, and poverty. But Hansie and Betsy are never forgotten in the providence of a loving God. They have the Book! So do we. And the Holy Spirit has something to say to us that can make God's Word a livable proposition in our lives.

The original Hansie and Betsy have slept these past four centuries in a German graveyard, awaiting everything the Book promised them while they lived. But in their own day they needed God and his Word to get them through their tedious, pointless hours.

I never want to forget how much their struggles resemble my own.

So, I raise the chalice to God's Holy Spirit, the author of God's Book, to these, my long-dead sisters. This is the Holy Spirit's simple Word, the Bible, the grand book—the good book—the God Book!

7

AWAKENING AND EVANGELISM

In 1742, many parishes in Scotland were visited with times of refreshing. The parish of Cambuslang, near Glasgow, then under the pastoral charge of William McCulloch, was one of the first to be visited. After he had preached for about a year on the nature and necessity of regeneration, he was requested by about ninety heads of families to give them a weekly lecture. Prayer-meetings were formed; and one after another, at a length fifty in the same day, came to him in distress of mind. After this, such was their thirst for the Word of God, that he had to provide them a sermon almost daily; and before the arrival of George Whitefield three hundred souls had been converted.[1]

JAMES BUCHANAN

Twice in my life I have seen religious awakenings close at hand.

Only months after the famed "Saskatoon Revival," I visited Saskatoon, Saskatchewan. A close friend of mine had played a leading role in that drama that proclaimed itself throughout the evangelical world. This friend told me of a series of evangelistic meetings that were set to occur in a small church. But all too soon revival leaders judged the church much too small to accommodate the ever-growing crowd. The meeting moved to a larger church and then finally to the 2,000-seat civic auditorium. Admittedly, the Canadian facility didn't approach the size of a Texas stadium, but still, given its context, it was quite large. And the final services of the revival found it packed—numerically remarkable, considering that the church in which they began had less than two hundred members.

As it has been in every other place where I've seen it happen, so it was in Saskatoon. The Canadians became one in experiencing a "post-revival stupefaction." They all felt awed by the Spirit's visitation, to such an extent that they became misty-eyed as they talked about the meeting and its impact on them. They lived in awe of the firestorm that forever altered their perception of God.

I also visited the Asbury College Campus in Wilmore, Kentucky, not too long after a different visitation of God. Once again I felt that community's reverence for the Holy Spirit and an exuberant willingness to talk about it. These participants likewise felt mystified as to the visitation's uncanny impact on the school and on their lives. No two of them described it alike. It should not have surprised me, for the best visitations of God leave everyone agreeing that something wonderful has happened—but no two of them explain his coming in the same way.

The "Asbury Revival" seems to have come about something as follows. Toward the end of a most ordinary—some said dry—chapel service, one student rose to ask another student to forgive him for the wrong he had done him. The aggrieved student stood to accept his apology, and then the two students made their way to the altar of the college chapel. All too soon two others joined them, and then two more, then four, then fifty. Soon the altar overflowed with scores of students. They came and went over the next six weeks—sometimes a hundred, sometimes a thousand—but never did the altar run dry.

Then the joy began to spread. The Spirit of renewal gradually passed out of Wilmore, Kentucky, to other campuses worldwide. The revival spread with a kind of joy the world has yet to quit talking about.

THE EBB AND FLOW OF THE SPIRIT'S REALITY

Christianity was born in Acts 2, when the Holy Spirit fell in wind and fire on the disciples. An awakening took place. It was as if the world had fallen asleep to all that really mattered and then suddenly awoke. Awoke? To what? To the larger purposes of God! To the vision that God would one day rule the universe and that Jesus would stand at the end of time to reign over his peaceable kingdom. But until that day and the close of history, the Holy Spirit would appear throughout Christian history to show us what the coming kingdom would look like when it did arrive.

During awakenings, God announces his presence to us with ultimate vitality. These periods usually arise because we who believe have somehow lost the vibrancy of our faith. We may still believe intellectually in the great truths of the gospel, but we might have lost our exuberance of those truths. Faith in such cases often becomes so matter-of-fact that it seems utterly mundane. Into this stolid matrix of religious blahs, someone enters the community bearing a warm and fresh experience with God.

Awakenings usually come and go, defying anyone's ability to predict the moment of their arrival. Within my parish we often felt the mysterious ebb and flow of God's presence. We all knew the cyclical nature of the Spirit's visitations—we knew he would return again, when the time was right. But his coming always occurred when some in our church welcomed his presence. The Holy Spirit of God seemed as eager for these visitations as were the most devout among us.

We must not see these trysts of glory as the product of anything less than God's furious desire to love us, meeting our hunger to worship him. Yet we must not go to church only because we feel compelled to seek the Spirit. This compulsion can degenerate into a neurosis that causes us to "hype" our joy rather than merely waiting for him to show up and give it to us. This can lead to the false notion that the Spirit shows up only to indulge us in some grand and giddy display, so we can lollygag in vast fields of trumped-up emotion.

Whenever the Spirit comes, he is bent on showing us the living Christ. We may experience emotion as Christ becomes real to us, but to pursue the Spirit only for the emotive thrill he brings turns the adoration of Christ into mere entertainment.

We are to be adorers of Christ, moment by moment, day

in and day out. As this becomes our continual preoccupation, our worship services will challenge us to change and call all people to Christ. This becomes customary in the church when Christians commit themselves to honest worship.

Still, awakenings are special. These warm seasons resemble Pentecost in their impact. A sense of wind and fire comes with a high incidence of conversions and confession. These special visitations may last a few weeks or even a few months. But they always ebb and sometimes leave us feeling unfulfilled, like January's drab reply to Christmas.

Yet as the Spirit withdraws, the church knows it is in no danger of losing the Spirit forever. The church and the Spirit are rather like lovers who treasure their special times of closeness, but never abandon the romance, even during periods of more matter-of-fact faith.

I found in our church that these times of "high awakening" often came as the result of the most extraordinary work of the Spirit. For instance, one evening in 1984, a young man in our church sat in the den of his very beautiful home. He looked out through the windows and saw a woman sitting in the den of the house next to his. This woman had been his neighbor for some time, and yet he had never spoken to her about Christ. Feeling guilty over this failure, he went next door to begin to talk to her. As a result, he convinced her of her need for Christ and she became a Christian.

She came to church the next Sunday and actually came forward to announce her conversion at the altar in our church. After the service she asked if I would talk to her husband about Christ; I agreed. During that visit in their home, he also came to faith in Christ. He came forward at the end of the next service and publicly acknowledged his faith. After the service he asked me to talk to his grown son, an attorney in our city. He, too, became a Christian. On the following Sunday, the son came forward to announce his newfound joy in Christ.

When the father saw his son making his way down the aisle, he got up from his seat and met him halfway down the aisle, in front of nearly two thousand members who saw the unfolding of a very emotional pageant. Nothing feels quite so emotionally involving as a father and son meeting at a church altar in tearful embrace. In their tears was born an era of utter revival that must have lasted for nearly two months. During those eight weeks, the church added more than a hundred new members into the fellowship, many of them from desperate and needy circumstances. Families found healing from dysfunction as they committed themselves to Christ. And all of the membership became committed to attending church to see what would happen next. After all, who would dare miss a service whose very existence called the world to a new order of things?

This is one way the Spirit comes, in the exotic nearness of a wonderful awakening.

NEW BIRTH, THE GRAND MIRACLE

At the heart of every awakening people join their lives to Christ for the first time. I have yet to see any authentic awakening where people are not born again.

One season of awakening in our church arrived when a boyhood chum of mine, whom we shall call Alex, moved to the town where I pastored. I hadn't seen him in years and felt most glad to have him back once again in my circle of friends. But the joy of our reunion dimmed when Alex told me that he had cancer and was not expected to live long. In talking about

Christ with him, I discovered that he was not a man of faith, and yet a man terribly in need of faith. So I found myself praying with him as he trusted Christ to be the Lord of his life. During his final weeks, I spent many hours with him and committed myself to giving him spiritual support as much as possible.

I was with him the day he died and actually held his hand and prayed for him as he entered eternity. I summoned the nurse to tell her that Alex had just passed away. As I made my way out of the room, the nurse entered the room with an attending physician. I nodded to them both and left the room on my way out of the hospital. But I had not gotten very far down the corridor when I heard someone call my name. When I turned back in the direction of Alex's room, I saw the doctor who had just accompanied the nurse into his room.

"Excuse me," said the doctor.

"Yes," I replied.

"Were you this man's pastor?" the doctor asked.

"Indeed," I replied.

"Can you, sir, tell me whether this man knew Christ as his Savior?"

"I can," I said. "I led him to faith in Christ some months ago."

"Oh, thank you," he said, "I feel so bad. I have been his physician for several months and I never asked him if he knew Christ as his Savior."

We parted and I continued making my way out of the hospital. Then suddenly I sensed the leadership of the Spirit and turned back toward Alex's room. When I found the physician issuing the death certificate, I said to him, "Excuse me, sir, but I've been visiting people in this hospital for years and I have met a lot of physicians here, but I can't ever remember a single one of them ever telling me they felt guilty for not having led anyone to Christ. If ever you had time, I would count it a privilege to take you to lunch." I gave him my card. The lunch we agreed to share became the first of our many visits. Eventually the doctor and I formed a life-long friendship. This man, more than anyone I can think of, awakened my own hunger for the ministry of the Holy Spirit to become central in my life.

When Alex came forward in our church, we met at the altar and his need for God so nourished my own that we experienced a long period of awakening, resulting in glory for the entire church. I soon realized that his need to see people like Alex come to faith was a need I shared. Out of Alex's conversion came a period of awakening that saw a great many people converted. A kind of euphoria resulted, for those who became believers found a compelling need to tell others.

Why? What brought it all on? New converts often feel a euphoria that fixes itself on Christ, making them unable to keep silent. They bear testimony to all they have discovered, their testimony frequently resulting in a dramatic season of widespread confession—"show and tell." A new reality possesses them, a reality so overwhelming that it carries them into the mystery of godliness and on into the heart of his daily, transforming nearness. This is the meaning of awakening: daily, transforming nearness.

If I must assign a value to the conversion activities of the Holy Spirit (for his values to the congregation are nearly uncountable and always varied), I would definitely speak of it as his transforming nearness. Wherever he comes, the world about him changes—but none of these changes seem more dramatic than when he redeems us. He transforms all in the miracle of new birth. But it never stops with that event. He goes on changing us for the rest of our lives and those changes, in time, completely recreate us.

THE CAPRICE OF THE GREAT VISITATIONS

One thing must be said of the Spirit: He does not come merely for the price of either our anticipation or our predictions. The Holy Spirit is a person. He has a mind of his own. He will do what he will do. He will visit us how and when he likes. How he comes is as varied as the individuality of our needs.

Unfortunately, we often try to prescribe the manner of his coming by forcing him to manifest himself in some "churchy" way. Some consider his coming authentic only if his arrival causes them to speak in tongues or worship him in the singing of contemporary choruses. Yet he may visit an Episcopal Church with an insight and majesty that would seem inappropriately "high-church" to one who believes his coming must always issue in *glossolalia*.

I always feel reluctant to mention the following quality of the Spirit, for it makes me seem less than a devout believer in intercessory prayer. But however fervently we may pray, God has his own agenda for our lives and our world. God will do what he will do, when and where he wants to do it. He does not have to check in with our prayer agenda. Furthermore, he may surprise us with good things, unasked for, surprising us at how very good these things are. It is like when we receive a wonderful and surprising gift from a friend on no special day of our lives, and for no special reason except as a reflection of our friendship. In such a way we receive the serendipities of God. The Holy Spirit ever surprises us with wonderful gifts that come from God at unexpected seasons of our lives.

I think this is often true of awakenings. Several times in the life of our local church, God sent us a great indulgence in his presence that surprised us all. At none of those times had I been praying for an awakening. Nor had any other group in our church. The Holy Spirit simply had a surprise visitation for us and we got lost in the immensity of his coming.

Not only this, but I have seen such spontaneous awakenings in other contexts to unsuspecting people. I can remember a campus revival at a religious student center at a state university. The attendance between Monday and Friday grew so exponentially (from a hundred to a thousand) that we could do nothing but feel amazed as students by the hundreds entered into faith in Christ.

I remember a missionary gathering in Latin America, where the numbers of missionaries and natives grew so much that by the end of the week, the packed building forced hundreds to gather on the lawn outside the church to listen intently as believers found strength and many unbelievers came to faith in Christ. Did we pray for these things? No. The Spirit surprised us. He came. And all things became wonderful.

I have seen his coming, even more wonderful, in places like Saskatoon or Asbury. Of course, people prayed; but perhaps, not for the coming of the Spirit. He just seemed to come on his own. It seemed he had come as a smile from some gleeful moment of God's caprice.

Why should God not have a mind of his own? He will come where and when he wants to. After all, the wind blows wherever it pleases, but you cannot tell from where it comes or to where it goes. Yet we do need to say that he never surprises us with his presence where he is unwelcome.

I love him for this one great quality of his love: his caprice. I don't think we should view this caprice as a whim, for God is not whimsical. It is not caprice as touches anything haphazard in the character of God. All that God does he does well, in a way wholly consistent with his purposes. But does he think at odd angles, as we petty humans view it? It may appear that way.

Yet it is this apparent caprice that makes his coming so wonderful. In the middle of the most mundane days, he suddenly appears among us, redeeming the world and calling us to a feast of joy where the fare only moments before seemed too thin to nourish us. Wind and Fire can then inhabit every drab season, making even the morose moments of our lives a theater of praise.

AWAKING TO THE GLORY OF GOD

To awake to God is to become instantly aware of our obligation of obedience. His sudden coming to us should always spur the question, "Lord, what wilt thou have me to do?" Remember the first words that Saul of Tarsus spoke after his Damascus road experience: "who are you, Lord?" His very use of the word "Lord" spoke implicitly of his subservience (Acts 9:5, NIV).

So in a way, awakening is more than awareness; it is submission. Never has a person come alive in Christ without agreeing almost immediately to surrender to whatever God has for that person. We wake up to God and to our need to obey him.

Holy Spirit breathe on me,
Till I am all thine own,
Until my will is lost in thine,
To live for thee alone.

As if to speak of the joy that accompanies the obedience
of awakening, another hymn says:

Trust and obey, for there's no other way,
To be happy in Jesus but to trust and obey.

Obedience and our awakening go hand in hand.

But to awaken us to God is also to awaken us to the glory
of praise. It would be a serious mistake to write a book on the
Holy Spirit without including a generous section on praise, for
praise is one of the Holy Spirit's key agendas in our lives. The
Holy Spirit wants us to glorify God. Praise is our warm privilege. Which of us, having received his grace, would not want to
glorify his name? He is, after all, the Son of God and our Savior. The Holy Spirit exists to call to our minds every aspect of
our Savior's work on the cross, his resurrection and exaltation,
his infilling and his coming again.

Is this important to Jesus? Of course! Praise forms a bond
between ourselves and our Savior and causes our Savior to
reach out to us as we reach up to him. But praise really reflects
our need, not God's. Jesus could go on living without our
praise; we cannot. We *must* praise him or we begin to die in-
wardly. A magnificent change occurs to us whenever we begin
to praise.

First, praise causes us to awake to God, because it frees us
from ourselves. We are very much addicted to our own ego. We

serve and love ourselves too much. But in praise, our heavenly focus frees us from our bondage to self-love. Once we get free of the necessity to enshrine ourselves at the center of all things, Jesus gets a chance to move into the spotlight. And when he becomes central in our lives, we have a chance to serve a higher agenda than our own. I know of no one who, having been set free in Christ, has contempt for praise.

Second, praise delivers us from a critical spirit. I have often gone into church with a huge spiritual chip on my shoulder. I do not brag about this; I confess it in shame. Who can say why any of us goes to church in a mad mood? Maybe we got up on the wrong side of the bed. Maybe we're sweltering from earlier emotional hangovers, over things gone wrong at work. Maybe a family member's comment on the way to church has drenched us in self-pity or made us angry. But there we sit in the presence of God, snarling and growling.

I have found on such mornings that nothing suits me. I find things misspelled in the worship bulletin. A woman in the choir has over-dyed her hair. The alto soloist sounds too nasal and the preacher should have studied more before coming out to preach.

Then the praise begins! Dumb songs! Listen how the choir mumbles the songs. Listen how the associate pastor splits every infinitive. Look at how little the man in the next row put in the offering plate; he ought to feel ashamed.

More praise! And now, somehow, church doesn't seem quite as dumb as it did when we first took our place in the pew. The more we sing, the better the over-dyed lady in the choir looks. Finally, she doesn't look bad at all. Gradually the church seems better and all things offensive look tolerable.

But why? Because we are being changed. That's what

praise does to us. It scrapes away our negative spirits and replaces them with a smile and a better attitude.

There is a sense in which we "fake it 'till we make it." In practicing a happier mood, we somehow become happier people. It really is easier to act our way into a new way of thinking than to think our way into a new way of acting. Or more positively put: it is easier to praise ourselves into a new attitude, than to attitude ourselves into a new way of praise.

MOVING TOWARD CONSTANT RENEWAL

Awakening is the act of coming out of sleep or lethargy so that we may infuse our lives with a greater, spirited vitality. We need to do this until such vitality becomes a way of life. The church should remain in a constant state of renewal. Our own personal awakenings must occur every morning of our lives.

Of course, I do not want to imply that we need to go to sleep so that we may experience an invigorating awakening! We are too prone toward a sleepy spirituality as it is. But we do need to experience genuine Sabbaths in which we cease our furious activities and invite our souls into seasons of godly rest and renewal. Then from these Sabbaths we can enter the world as disciples made alive for the work of bringing the world to Christ. Best of all, these awakenings will bring us a new kind of exhilaration. Wonderful things never before seen will adorn our lives. Glory will gild our days with praise.

8

COUNSEL

The Spirit blows where he will. Is there a freedom of the Spirit with regard to what the Word has affirmed and still affirms? Would any of us be able to reject the excellent question asked by John Ruskin: "Who knows where it will please God to let down his ladder?" God is free to intervene ubi et quando— *where and when he pleases.*[1]

YVES M.J. CONGAR

Brother Lawrence of the Resurrection once wrote to a nun to advise her on how to navigate the unfamiliar and treacherous passages of life. "Again I say, let us go into these waters ourselves . . . because not to advance in the spiritual life is to go back. But those on whom the Holy Spirit has breathed, go forward even when they sleep."[2]

Those of us on whom the Holy Spirit has breathed, have the Counselor, whom Brother Lawrence calls, "the Lord who sleeps therein." The Spirit's office of counselor, the most interior office of the Trinity, counsels us from inside our souls.

Counselor is one of the most meaningful names of the Holy Spirit. The word Counselor implies that God is an ever-available help for the needy times of our lives. Which of us has not found ourselves in such desperate extremes that we have felt bereft of hope and direction? When we descend to such helplessness, the Holy Spirit stands ready and available to serve as our celestial navigator to help us find our way through the misty passages of life. The Spirit serves as our pilot, guiding the way through the inky seas of our depression and the bleak lagoons of our loss.

On the morning of September 11, 2001, Tom McGuinness kissed his wife Cheryl goodbye and left for the airport, heading toward his job as the copilot on American Airlines Flight 11, bound for Los Angeles. Cheryl could not know, nor could Tom, that in less than two hours his life would end in an explosion of fire at the World Trade Center in New York City. As Cheryl negotiated the rough seas of turmoil in the days following Tom's funeral, she encountered again and again the counsel of God's Holy Spirit, who gave her gold in the form of these wonderful promises of God. She confessed her need and the Spirit's counsel: "Her prayers were mostly cries for the Lord to hold her, comfort her and strengthen her in her new role as a widow and a single mom. 'I would groan to God on my knees, knowing he hears my prayers,' Cheryl says, 'Isaiah 65:24, proclaims, *Before they call I will answer; while they are still speaking I will hear.* I still take comfort in that.' "[3]

How each of us, like Cheryl, needs Brother Lawrence's Lord who lives within!

THE SPIRIT'S COUNSEL AND THE LAUGHTER OF GOD

Every sunrise forces us to face up to James's unpleasant truth: "You do not even know what will happen tomorrow" (James 4:14, NIV). Which of us does not feel baffled here and there by our purpose and reason to be? But on no morning of our lives do we need to wake up without the confidence that the Spirit has all things under control. Our victory through the Holy Spirit is certain and we may give God the glory for our triumph.

Yet despite the Spirit's reality and presence, we sometimes come face-to-face with the fact that, at any moment, life may become instantly unmanageable. When our eye fixates on our helplessness, we may find ourselves saying, "Oh, that I had a friend counselor—someone who might lift my torn soul and point the way through the tangle of circumstances in which I now find myself."

In a sense, this desperate soliloquy is blasphemous. To have the Holy Spirit ever within us and yet long for him—as though he is not at hand—is an odd denial. It is an insult to Christ's promise, "I will never leave you nor forsake you" (Heb. 13:5, KJV). It contradicts Jesus' promise to us: "It is for your good I am going away. Unless I go away the counselor will not come to you . . ." (John 16:7, NIV).

This is the most remarkable thing about the counsel of the indwelling Spirit: those who seem to abound with the most obvious joy, do not have less frequent troubles. In fact, just the opposite seems true. Those with the most joyous lives have often wept their way to the inner Counselor. Laughter among people of real faith does not indicate that they are strangers to affliction. The truly joyous often have lived on the edge of an abyss where they have had to face the glare of despair and learn the laughter of God.

All things really are subject to Christ's joy. Laughter is more eternal than the human predicament. Marlene Le Fever says that one little girl in her Sunday school class said of the God of John 3:16, "whosoever believeth in him should not perish but have 'ever-laughing life.' "[4] If she corrupted the verse, she certainly did so in a worthy fashion.

Do you think this too frivolous a definition? Even as I write these words, I am grieving over the martyrdom of a wonderful physician. I have sought the laughter of God, but indeed I find it hard to find in the present moment. The West felt shock when the news hit that Islamic extremists had killed Dr. Martha Myers. I confess I found little reason to celebrate the cruelty of life as laughter. I can still see Martha, with whom I had prayed so fervently during my brief time in Yemen, as she ministered to the abused Moslem women she so loved. I can see her big SUV, filled with burqa-clothed women, hauling them to and from the clinic. This doctor, who might have made a fortune in an American career, felt content to deliver babies to all the oppressed women who came to her. She would deliver a baby for five dollars if they could afford it, for nothing if they couldn't.

Now she is with the Lord she loved, martyred through the treachery of those she had befriended. Some four years ago she wrote Dr. Dan Crawford and me a letter rich with the account of her faith in God. But as a part of the letter she included these words:

> I praise him for the good, close friends, he has given me . . . I'm learning over the years why my little student-language helper used the word *friend* much more discriminately than I . . . He told me, "Don't think just because you work with those people in the operating room they are your friends . . . They have lied about us to the police . . . stolen personal hospital goods, eaten in my home and came back to rob it . . ." It must have hurt when Jesus came unto his own and his own received him not. When his own family wasn't sure He was in his right mind because he was so involved in his work . . . Everyday there were people trying to catch him at his words, to cause him problems with the government, by twisting his truth into lies . . . the things we did not know or refused to believe about our friends and workers he must have been aware of still faithful to pray and love and care till the day he was betrayed . . . even the day he died, bleeding . . . and grieving for the wasted life he would gladly have ransomed.[5]

I swelter these days under the remembrance of a beautiful life snuffed out by the cruel world she wanted so much to save. In my despair I found no justification for this, no answer to be given. Can the Holy Spirit teach me to laugh in such dark moments? It seems not.

Yet I remember Dr. Myers, after an earlier kidnapping and release, laughing so generously about the experience that we all tended to laugh with her. We laughed, I think, because she made us believe those words of F.B. Meyers: "The tears of life belong to its interlude, not its finale."[6] God will ultimately wipe away all tears. Then laughter will be the counsel of the Holy Spirit, enduring long after all crying has ceased.

The Railway of Our Obedience

Most people never see the Holy Spirit as an ever-present, non-forsaking Counselor. Thus they work hard at trying to think out things for themselves. Often they seek psychotherapy as a way to arrive at paid advice, in this way making God the last resort in trying to solve the enigmas of life. But in the end, only the counsel of God can lift us from our despair and once again set our derailed lives back on the track.

I often think of the Spirit's leadership as a "track to run on." I grew up in Oklahoma where my childhood home stood only about a half a block from the Atchison, Topeka and Santa Fe Railroad. I used to love to go and sit down by the railroad track and watch the trains go by. I would sit for hours beside the tracks, watching the huge, steel dragons slither by my home. These "puffer bellies" drew a hundred cars of Oklahoma wheat as they passed. I would often ask myself, "What is the strange force and mystery that drives this heavy iron monster with such strong intention to a distant city?"

I remember asking my mother once, "Where do these tracks go?" And I recall her very clearly saying, "Well, they go to Los Angeles, Houston, or Chicago." I remember thinking how wonderful it felt to live in a little dusty community beside the steel rails that ended in such distant and exotic places I had never visited.

I used to say to my mother, "It must take a talented man to drive a train all the way to Houston." "No," she would say, "It takes only an ordinary man with a bit of training. The train goes to Houston or to Los Angeles, or to Chicago because that's where the tracks go. If the train ever tried to be unfaithful to those tracks, it would never arrive at those far-away places. It must follow the tracks."

The metaphor has stuck with me all these years. It strikes me that if a Christian would take the most direct way to the will of God, he must follow the rails of obedience. And it is the Holy Spirit who guides us in this matter.

LAY ASIDE YOUR GRIEF

The Holy Spirit first came to the New Testament church at the end of ten long days, lonely days charged with despair. The Savior had returned to heaven and they knew that until he returned to keep his promise of John 14:15–16, they would never find any alleviation for their grief.

But the Comforter came.

He always comes when his church seems locked in grief. He comes to say, "Lay aside your sorrow. Do not dwell on how you will achieve this or that. Never let your grief paralyze you in any aspect of the life you ought to be achieving."

Jesus wants us to miss him and he wants us to long for our reunion with him—but he does not want our grief over his absence in this world to paralyze us to the place where we cannot minister to others. He has sent the Holy Spirit to walk along side us. Christ has work to be done and the Spirit will empower us to do it.

I've lost only a few people to death in my long life. My wife can say the same thing. In both our families, our loved ones seem genetically destined to live a long time. But I have lost my mother and her loss has left a great hole in my system of meaning. She has been gone for twenty-five years, but I still think from time to time, *I wonder what she would say about this?* or *I wonder what her direction would be in such and such a matter?*

That's exactly why the Holy Spirit came, because we all have those "WWJD" moments when we are forced to ask ourselves, "What would Jesus do?" The Holy Spirit is there to give us counsel, to inform us exactly what Jesus would do. And he would say to us, "Don't grieve, but remember Paul's advice: Don't grieve as those who have no hope" (1 Thess. 4:13). We do have hope, a double hope. First, we know we shall see him again. And second, we have the solid counsel of the Holy Spirit to guide us through all our shattering times of darkness and uncertainty.

When we get honest we must admit that grief has a way of paralyzing us. In spite of Jesus' promise that he would send the Holy Spirit to save us from grief's paralysis, I've known young widows who sat in a dark room for hours, shackled to their grief. They refused to unshutter the windows of their despair to let in any light. And yet these hours of lost living produced nothing. They simply filled in the moments of their own lives, pushing them along toward their own death.

Part of us seems to enjoy the deadly game of grief's paralysis. I've seen this bent psychology destroy the living mates of people who had enjoyed a long marriage. Both of them die, yet only one is buried. The other fills up the purposeful moments they might have known by making the rest of their life a long day's journey into night. Such grief paralyzes them by placing their rocking chair on the edge of the grave. It is not a purposeful place to rock, yet it gratifies them in a morose sort of way.

When Jesus went back to heaven, his followers loved him so much they might have sat to grieve their loss and achieve nothing. But they took a more meaningful pathway through their grief: they entered into prayer for ten days, seeking his return in the coming of the Holy Spirit. And when the Holy Spirit came, he came in such power that it obliterated all their grief and launched the Kingdom of God in a furor of excitement. Furthermore, when Jesus came again through his Spirit, the glory of his Spirit so impacted their hearts that nothing remained but to follow him in complete trust.

FORGET THE CLOCK

All of our lives we serve the clock. In our own day it has become a frantic business to run hither and thither, always trying to meet the thousands of deadlines that crowd in upon us every week. In this hurried madness, no one has time to notice anyone else. On and on the clocks' mad tocks drive us ever forward, crying, "Serve me faster! Don't look up! Be a workaholic!"

Enblazened on the face of many old clocks was the little Latin phrase, *Tempus Fugit*, "time flies." Time flies indeed and the Bible tells us that we don't get a lot of it. In fact, we get only "three score years and ten." Time is not to be wasted, for God has business with us and all meaning lies in our ability to get it done.

I teach homiletics in the seminary and young preacher wannabes are forever asking me, "How long should I preach?" To tell a preacher how long he should preach is usually a waste of breath. Yet for the most part, preachers should not preach a long time. After all, the head cannot absorb more than the seat can endure. Neither, however, should the sermon ever serve the clock. The sermon must be the guided work of the Holy Spirit; it must belong to him. It fascinates me that every time an awakening comes, services tend to lengthen. The clock is not there to control us, but to inform us of the passing of our lives. The clock ought to remind us to take charge of our lives.

Wonderful things happen when we lay aside the clock. In other books I have spoken about *otium sanctum*, or "holy leisure." Holy leisure was that state in which all saints wished to approach God, because they realized that God cannot be known while we keep one eye fastened on him and the other on a timetable. We cannot move into the presence of God as though we could favor him only with a certain amount of time—and when that time was up, God's appointment was over. When we have conquered our slavery to the clock, we will approach God through the *otium sanctum*.

But how is this different from any important human relationship? We would never have people over for dinner and specify that they are to arrive at 4:30 sharp, for they are expected to leave promptly at 6:30. It doesn't occur to us to keep our best social engagements with time constraints set on either end of the event. Yet we very much live that way in our ordinary lives, and we often run our church services that way.

This has led us to bizarre forms of relating to God through the Holy Spirit. We run into the prayer room—into the very throne of God—slam down our prayer demands and run out again so that we can be on time for our next appointment. But the Holy Spirit wants us to know that God is not some fast-food supplier of our "McPrayerlife." He is the unhurried Jehovah who treasures those wonderful moments of leisure that we freely give him.

LAY ASIDE YOUR PROPRIETY IN FAVOR OF LIFE

Every time the Holy Spirit gets involved in our affairs, wonderful things happen. He generally challenges us to lay aside all the social constraints that rule our lives. Those social constraints we often call propriety.

Propriety is that scale of values that tells us what or what is not proper. But this propriety can often govern us in ways foreign to our true enjoyment of an occasion. This is not altogether bad, because propriety can keep down many bizarre forms of anti-social behavior. But propriety can also grow stiff and unavailing.

We often cherish those times when, as young people, life gets away from us. The wonderful times of life tend to govern us. Perhaps we stay out too late and our parents chide us because good kids don't stay out too late. Or we find ourselves shucking the rules of propriety because they get in the way of a wonderful time. The good times of growing up sometimes cause us to forget all propriety. We ditch our captivity to "what will people think?" We quit caring about how we might appear to others. We exalt the joy of hanging loose. Sometimes these moments of freedom entice the Holy Spirit to come into our midst in special power. It is then that we begin to experience warm and wonderful things we should not otherwise have known had we insisted on serving the Baals of cold propriety.

One of the first issues that stuns our "high-church" propriety is the issue of healing. We evangelicals can become a little nervous when someone calls in the Holy Spirit to heal. Sometimes we think that television evangelists have gone overboard in selling prayer cloths or dramatic antics. We feel a desire to disassociate ourselves from such activities.

The more proper Christians also feel offended at the impropriety of "spirit slayings." I have no idea what this practice generally means, but some Christians believe that when God comes too near the human soul, that soul cannot stand the nearness of his glory. The very closeness of God becomes a power that slays all those who dare to approach too near it.

Chet Raymo, an astronomer, has written a wonderful book called *The Soul of the Night*.[7] The book is delightful to read even for lay astronomers, but at the front of the book he reminds his readers that the stars we love to study are not merely the little pinpoints of fixed light they appear to be. They are not diamond studs stamped immovable and cold on the dark velvet firmament of night. The stars are flaming suns, and were we to approach them too directly, the roar of nuclear fire that sustains them would destroy us. Seen at a comfortable distance they can warm an earth and make life possible. But seen too close, they become raging fire that none can control and whose hydrogen flame would obliterate and not enhance life.

So we have the Holy Spirit. He exists in our world to bring God near to us, to make life possible. Still, those, who approach him too closely, say the cable evangelists, must experience him as a God whose fiery nearness slays.

As Moses climbs the mountain as recorded in the book of Exodus, the Lord informs him that he will see the back of God but not the front, because the front of God would cause him to fall over dead. No man can see God and live, God tells Moses. The whole idea of spirit slaying, as it has come to be practiced, seems to be that the nearest glory of God is so intense that mortals cannot stand the fullness of his presence, and so must fall unconscious.

The spectacle of such an episode occurring on television

to long lines of ardent believers, leaves evangelicals more misunderstood by a skeptical culture than they would like to be.
But let us ask ourselves: should an all-powerful God never do
anything that astounds us? Many who see this, of course, do
not feel so much astounded as turned off by the show-biz
histrionics. Still, we must further ask, "Is it a mere issue of in-
jured propriety, or do we really believe that such things never
happen?" Those who believe that everything God does must fit
some code of propriety, it seems to me, are in for a long, dry
ride. This kind of spirituality never quickens the heart or moves
the spirit into deeper worship. I do not advocate that we all become slayers in the spirit or be slain in the spirit. But I do advocate that each of us needs to make a place for God to do
things that escape our understanding. Only such a God could
ever bring a sense of newness or the force of worship into our
predictable lives.

WESLEY'S WARMTH OF GOD'S FIRE

All of us, I suppose, know well the story of John Wesley and how
he came to America to begin a work among the Indians. Yet
Wesley's work to convert the natives didn't go too well, for he
did not feel converted himself. "I came to Georgia to convert the
Indians," he lamented, "but who shall convert John Wesley?"

Wesley hungered for the fire of God. Coming and going
to America, he had traveled aboard ship with some Moravians.
Twice during storms at sea he noticed these people as they
knelt to pray on the deck of the ship. When others around
them panicked at the fierceness of the storms, the Moravians
seemed most at peace. Wesley spoke to them about the warmth
of God's fire and himself developed a hunger for God's fire.

I suspect this is a form of godly addiction for which most lovers of God hunger. Even the most intellectual Christians must have a time when they quit massaging their brains long enough for something mysterious and inexplicable to happen to their hearts.

When Wesley finally returned to England, he passed a Moravian chapel and saw these pious souls inside worshipping. When he entered the chapel, he felt "his heart strangely warmed." And from this new warmth proceeded the great Wesleyan revivals.

Wesley modeled for us those wonderful things that come to us when we begin to seek the warmth of God's fire. We become willing to lose our designation as "God's frozen chosen." We willingly scathe dead propriety and the arctic atmosphere of rigid worship to find again the renewing warmth of God's Holy Spirit.

God encourages us to try to build a warmth in worship services by which the lost feel intrigued to come to the fire of God, where this fire is given free reign to burn in the lives of those willing to be redeemed.

One thing is sure: once we have experienced this warmth, we can never again feel content with our colder, more frigid kinds of worship. So many churchmen in our day have left more formal denominations in favor of those that offer a feeling that God really is involved and that the warmth of God's fire can bleed through the devotion of those who love to worship.

CHERISH THE COMMUNITY OF MYSTERY

When we come into relationship with Christ, we understand that in the presence of the Spirit things happen that are too wonderful for ordinary minds to understand. This community of mystery in God most readily proclaims his best reality.

Why mystery? Because God in his fullness confronts us with things too rich to comprehend. Then God who invites us to attend this mystery attends our need. We must have the mystery, for the propriety which eliminates this mystery will in time eliminate the church.

Once the mystery is gone, so is the power of transformation. Transformation always appears mysterious. When people change, we can see that something has happened, for they seem different than they were. But we are at a loss to measure either the state they appear soon to achieve, or to identify the force that transformed them into something quite different from what they were. Yet only this mystery can change the church into a compelling center of intrigue.

The Holy Spirit often acts in ways that we cannot understand. His ways are always higher than our ways and his thoughts are always higher than our thoughts (Isaiah 55:9). Indeed, mystery may be defined as the gap between his reality and our understanding. But only where it fills the church with transformation do we find true Christianity.

This mystery is the fuel of revival. It is the invisible, inaudible, intangible glory of God. Where people struggle to explain, it dies, but where they revel in its unfathomable reality, they are born again.

How rich is this glory. We can be transformed by the mystery of the Holy Spirit! God is most powerful and we are most content when we find it far less important to understand God than merely to enjoy him.

PART III

THE
PLEASURE
OF THE
SPIRIT

꒰꒱

9

GRIEF

Don't grieve God. Don't break his heart. His Holy Spirit, moving and breathing in you, is the most intimate part of your life, making you fit for himself. Don't take such a gift for granted.

EPHESIANS 4:30,
THE MESSAGE

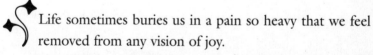Life sometimes buries us in a pain so heavy that we feel removed from any vision of joy.

I remember a Mr. Hardison who suffered a heart attack just as a Sunday morning service began. I had just entered the pulpit area to begin the service when this kindly man stood, began clawing at his collar, and promptly crumpled. I will never forget the look of shock that hit his wife's face as he fell. Immediately I moved to the pew where she sat and where her husband had collapsed. I prayed with her and tried to help her hold on to hope. Gradually, as the paramedics arrived and it became clear he had died, I felt the shuddering in her shoulders—the hopeless trembling—that provides an early sign of the despair that gives birth to grief.

Grief is a heavy emotion. It crushes us because the hurt we bear is too weighty to shrug off. Grieving is never the work of an instant. It dogs our attempt to feel good and unleashes the tears of our hopeless condition for whole seasons of our life. We had to remind Mrs. Hardison of the great promise: human beings are never alone in their brokenness. God too grieves. Paul said in Romans that when we grieve, the Spirit himself becomes our advocate and intercedes for us with groanings that cannot be uttered (Rom. 8:27). God grieves when we grieve.

But the person in the Godhead we are most likely to cause grief by our own willfulness is the Holy Spirit. Why? Because this is the person of the Godhead most intimately bound up in the important choices of our lives. He indwells our very souls, and from this inner place in our lives, our every act of disobedience inflicts pain.

BLASPHEMING VS. GRIEVING

Many equate the issue of grieving the Holy Spirit with blaspheming against the Holy Spirit. But they are unalike. Grieving the Spirit is never good, but it knows instant forgiveness when we come to God in confession. Blaspheming the Holy Spirit, on the other hand, the Bible calls the unforgivable sin. Jesus knew of only one unforgivable sin:

I tell you the truth, all the sins and blasphemies of men will be forgiven them. But whoever blasphemes against the Holy Spirit will never be forgiven; he is guilty of an eternal sin (Mark 3:28–29, NIV).

What did Jesus mean when he warned us against blaspheming the Holy Spirit? Some say, and I tend to agree with this interpretation, that to blaspheme the Holy Spirit is to continually say "no" to him as he pleads with us to let Jesus Christ be Lord in our lives. Certainly, such a serious view of refusing Christ admittance should enable us to understand how important it is to receive Jesus Christ. In other words, blaspheming the Holy Spirit is not merely a matter of saying "no" to God or even to Christ. It is to stand blatantly against the Holy Spirit, refusing his every entreaty that we allow him a place in our lives.

Unlike blasphemy, grieving the Holy Spirit is far simpler and more common than this. We may grieve the Holy Spirit by any act of self will. Every point of disobedience grieves the Holy Spirit.

An ancient cliché says, "Sin against God and the Son will forgive you. Sin against the Son and the Spirit will forgive you. But sin against the Spirit and none will forgive you." This tryptich may sound superficial, but its truth is real.

THE FEAR OF LOSING CONTROL

We are all born with an innate tendency toward self-preservation. We tend to turn away from risk. Anything that threatens our well-being and our absolute control over our lives, causes us to galvanize our resistance against the threat.

The fear of self-sacrifice possesses us all. For this reason, we quail to surrender to God. We fear to commit to anything or anyone beyond the narrow borders of ourselves, lest we lose control over our destiny.

Karl Gustav Jung said, "Fear of self-sacrifice lurks deep in every ego."[1] Somehow when we examine what it really means to give ourselves to Christ, we grow terrified of the surrender involved. Perhaps one of the things we most fear about falling victim to Alzheimer's syndrome is the loss of selfhood.

Why the terror? Because we see that as we lose our self-awareness we will lose all sense of our significance. By the time we reach adulthood, this great fear has set up camp in the middle of our lives.

Is there a way to avoid this fear of losing ourselves? Yes! By giving ourselves away. We cannot lose what we do not own. So if we have agreed to let God own our life, then the possibility of losing it no longer exists. Jesus said that dying is exactly what it takes to really live. Giving it away is the only way to keep it. Jesus said, "Whoever loses his life for my sake will find it" (Matt. 10:39, NIV). And the only way we can save our life is to yield it up to Jesus Christ.

GOD'S GREATEST DESIRE

God is a Spirit and they who worship him must do so in Spirit (John 5:24). Jesus believed that God was altogether Spirit. God is not the enemy of all things material; indeed, he pervades the world of material things. God is a Spirit at home throughout his created universe.

The only place ever closed to the all-pervasive Spirit of God is the human heart. Human will remains sovereign and we must either open our hearts to him of our own accord or the Holy Spirit will never enter them. Human will alone forbids God his right to inhabit our souls. The entire spiritual history of the human race since Eden has been the tale of the pursuing God seeking to regain the rebellious real estate of the human will.

Yet to own our hearts is God's greatest desire. No wonder Jesus spoke of blasphemy against the Spirit as our refusal to let the all-pervasive Spirit, who roams wide and free throughout the universe, invade our hearts! To forbid him access is to blaspheme. So why would we dare to blaspheme his love? Again, we fear the loss of ourselves. None of us mind giving a bit of our time to God—but our entire lives? We feel terrified by the notion of losing ourselves. Giving God complete control remains our chief terror. We fear losing our identity in the happy merger of ourselves with God.

GRIEF IS A SIN AGAINST LOVE

Grief is a "love" word. Ephesians 4:30 says, "Do not grieve the Holy Spirit" (NIV). When we refuse to obey God, we don't make God angry—we wound his great, loving heart. For God desires to be gracious and loving to us; he wants to prosper us and not to harm us, says Jeremiah. Therefore to refuse to obey him is to sin against earth's highest prize—the love of God. To sin against our Divine Lover is to grieve the Holy Spirit.

But why is it such a sin? It is a sin because it allows us to think we can partition God's great demands for us into a small corner of our lives. How foolish! How sinful! God will not stand for the partition of anything. Nor will he be content to live in a smaller circle of our wide obligations. He is one, and the Force behind the merger of all things into his solitary being and his single loving purpose. God wants to bring his intuitive purpose to the center of our lives. God would have you hear him say to you, "Listen up! There is no me and you—there is only us. I want no walls, no divisions. I want us to be one."

To rebel against God is to raise a wall in the very center of his love. Why would we ever throw up such barriers? Because love is the ultimate self-surrender. The diplomat Dag Hammarskjöld once said,

> I don't know Who—or what—put the question. I don't know when it was put. I don't even remember answering. But at some moment I did answer Yes to Someone—or Something—and from that hour I was certain that existence is meaningful and that, therefore, my life, in self-surrender, had a goal.[2]

Christians should crave such a wonderful preoccupation with this ultimate invasion of God. How wonderful to have been so loved!

And so what does conversion mean? Just this: there was one delightful moment when we became his, but not out of fear for our own displacement. We did it to enhance our existence with real significance. Now we are his. It is altogether a delightful idea that we have said "I do" to God and all we feared we would lose has now been accounted to us as gain. We were once empty, but now we are filled with his Holy Spirit. Now having discovered how much is ours, we are possessed with a narcotic desire to have ever more of his addictive love. Our desires have ripened into the fruit of obedient joy.

But what if we refuse him?

We grieve him. We wound his love.

We say no to the Father of yes.

GRIEF IS A FAILURE TO SURRENDER

We all feel a need to take charge of our private world. We all fear that any surrender of our souls would cause us to lose our personal mastery over our circumstances.

So, self-surrender confronts our every moment of choice. It scowls at every idea of yielding to God. Losing control threatens the meaning of our existence, causing us to want to ignore God's gentle tap on our shoulder, to set aside his incessant plea to let him take charge of our lives, and to live life on our own.

Still, our need to remain in charge lies always in second place to our need to be owned. Why is this? Who can say? But it seems to be so. Gerald May confesses our need and fear of surrender:

> We all have secrets in our hearts. I will tell you one of mine. All my life I have longed to say yes, to give myself completely, to some Ultimate Someone or Something. I kept this secret for many years because it did not fit the image I wanted to present—that of an independent, self-sufficient man. The desire to surrender myself had been at least partially acceptable when I was a child, but as a man I tried to put away childish things. When I became a physician, and later a psychiatrist, it was still more difficult to admit—even to myself—that something in me was searching for an ultimate self-surrender.[3]

Despite our terror in being owned by God, something else in us cries out for self-surrender. The terror of being owned finally gives rise to a greater fear: the terror of not being owned.

The very first naval flag of the colonists flew on December 3, 1775. On that day the flagship *Alfred* raised the first official American flag. The flag featured a simple but defiant banner that read, "Don't tread on me." To some degree, the flag expresses the center of our natural credo. And what is that American credo? In short, it is this: don't mess with my individuality. Don't try to shake me, don't try to touch me, don't try to remold or reform me. From the very outset of our existence, we cherish the idea that we are our own and that nobody has a right to meddle with our individual sovereignty. We pride ourselves on the idea of freedom that lies at the heart of the American spirit. *Don't tread on me.*

But the Spirit cries out that it is time to change flags. It is time for us to say, "Yes, don't tread on Jesus. Don't tread on the Holy Spirit." These are the true banners of the kingdom. We must always try to yield to God if we would avoid grieving the Holy Spirit. We must ever try to show a yielded spirit before God. Still, we find it difficult to let go of ourselves, to ease up in godly relaxation. And this failure to surrender, of course, grieves God.

What parents, especially parents of my age, cannot remember certain wonderful days when their children, who had been fighting them on some issue of obedience, suddenly yielded? To the glory of the child, two things happened. First, the parent felt pleased that the child finally grew in her maturity to the point where she could understand the nature of true wisdom. But an even greater thing happened. The mother felt pleased because she realized that her child had finally come to understand that her mother never wanted anything that wasn't good for the daughter in the first place.

Most family dysfunction probably arises from the feeling that the parents want something for the child that the child feels is not good for it. Not so! Neither in dysfunctional families, nor in our service to God. Yieldedness is always a wonderful thing. It accepts what God wants for us, which is the only good thing for us, anyway. Grief results from our failure to surrender to the good things God desires for us.

GRIEF WOUNDS OUR ALLEGIANCE TO GOD

Sometimes we enter the presence of God and salute the Holy Spirit without really meaning it. In fact, I suppose one of the things that so disgruntled the Old Testament prophets was that they noticed people going through empty religious activities devoid of content and meaning. I really believe that one grief guaranteed to wound the heart of God is to go through the motions of religiosity without any content in our spirituality.

We find one of the great stories from Scripture in the fifth chapter of Acts, embarrassingly near the day of Pentecost. Ananias and Sapphira desired to make a gift to the Holy Spirit and told the church that they had given everything, when in fact they gave merely a partial gift. What a false sacrifice! With his wife's full knowledge, Ananias kept back part of the money for himself and brought the rest of it and put it at the apostles' feet (Acts 5:1-2). The couple's real sin came when they told the church that they had given all the money they made from the sale of their property. On the spot God struck both dead for the sin of lying to the Holy Spirit. This deceitful pair didn't lie merely to the people of the congregation. As the writer of the book of Acts saw it, they lied to the Holy Spirit. They built a huge wall in the center of their allegiance to their heavenly Father.

Grief wounds the high allegiance that we ought to give to Jesus alone. And how do we inflict this wound? We do it when we make some statement or take some stand in the church just to let everyone know that we are good Christians. We set ourselves up for a fall when we join the church and affirm our faith too ostentatiously. We confess our faith superficially, and before long we may find ourselves acting in self-interest.

Grief always wounds the allegiance we ought to have given to our Father. The only way I know to keep from wounding our allegiance to him is to remember all that we owe God. This great debt should lead us to understand that we must do nothing partially for God—and above all, we must be honest in not claiming too much for our own sense of yieldedness.

GRIEF PLAYS LIGHT WITH MAJESTY

I believe that we grieve God when we do not respect God as God.

While sacrilege does not quite approach blasphemy against the Holy Spirit, it remains one of the highest sins. I truly believe that when people commit the sin of sacrilege, they take the highest dignity that could ever be known and subject it to the gutter. They bring God's high nature down to a crude expression of one sort or another. They do not respect God as God.

Jude labels these "I-am-all-for-me-and-none-for-God" disciples as filthy dreamers who, "defile the flesh, reject authority, and speak evil of dignitaries." Their worst sin? They "speak evil of whatever they do not know; and whatever they know naturally, like brute beasts, in these things they corrupt themselves." Jude says of these unsurrendered church leaders, "Woe to them! For they have gone in the way of Cain, have run greedily in the error of Balaam for profit, and perished in the rebellion of Korah." He describes these unyielded religious luminaries as "spots in your love feasts, while they feast with you without fear, serving only themselves. They are clouds without water, carried about by the winds . . . twice dead, pulled up by the roots; raging waves of the sea, foaming up their own shame: wandering stars for whom is reserved the blackness of darkness forever" (Jude 8-13, NKJV).

When Jude says that these sacrilegious religionists "speak evil of dignitaries," he means that they play lightly with the majesty of God. Surely this is a sin that grieves the Holy Spirit, because the Holy Spirit is the great defender and lover of Jesus Christ. The Spirit feels broken in grief when we will not magnify Christ, the sole object of his affection.

GRIEF MISTREATS OTHERS

The passage on "not grieving the Holy Spirit" comes in the middle of a paragraph and not at the beginning. The principle idea of the paragraph reveals itself in the title sentence, where Paul says, "Therefore each of you must put off falsehood and speak truthfully to his neighbor, for we are all members of one body" (Eph. 4:25, NIV).

Following this opening sentence, Paul denounces a great many sins, sticking at the center of his denunciation the sin of grieving the Holy Spirit. When you are irate don't go to bed while you're angry, he says (Eph. 4:26). Never give the devil a foothold in your life (Eph. 4:27). In 4:28 he says, Let him who has been used to stealing, quit stealing and get a job. Never let unwholesome or ungodly, vulgar words come out of your mouth (Eph. 4:29). Get rid of bitterness, anger, rage, brawling, slander, and every form of malice (Eph. 4:31).

Paul puts the issue of grieving the Holy Spirit right in the middle of these instructions on how we are to behave. What does this mean? It means that we as the people of God are to be concerned about every part of our morality. We will not grieve the Holy Spirit if we refrain from doing any of the things in this dreadful list of what disappoints God.

CALLED TO BE LOVERS OF GOD

There are many ways to grieve the Holy Spirit, but we need not focus on his displeasure. We would please God tremendously if we conditioned ourselves to become a giant "yes" before all that God demands of us. Then we would approach his every entreaty very positively, saying, "I will give my life uncompromisingly to Jesus Christ, to do my duty in loving him." And if we truly live up to that dictum, then most of the counsel of this chapter would become unnecessary.

We are called to be lovers of God, lovers of Jesus—obedient in every aspect. When we have mastered these very simple disciplines of the ready "yes," it will be impossible for us to grieve the Holy Spirit, for his pleasure will be ours. Our entire lives will be a grand yielding to better management.

10

RAPTURE

The fresh breath of the Spirit, too
has come to awaken latent energies
within the Church,
to stir up dormant charisms, and to
infuse a sense of vitality and joy.
It is this sense of vitality and joy
which makes the Church youthful and
relevant in every age,
and prompts her to proclaim joyously
her eternal message to each new epoch.[1]

POPE PAUL IV

The Holy Spirit has no interest in our merely being good. He desires to create a new nature within us. Yet we are not simple, passive creatures in whom he might work such a miracle. We have our own part to play in allowing him to implant this new nature. This involves a total revision of our personality that brings a life of new experience and inner joy.

When this inner joy reaches its most sublime point, it becomes a kind of rapture, an elation so uncontainable that it splashes color over our drab personalities. Worship—public and private—becomes our preoccupation. We find ourselves constantly absorbed in thinking of the greatness of God or the magnificence of Christ. This continual adoration awakens within us the Spirit's uncontainable joy. So effervescent is this joy that we who live in this other-worldly rapture sometimes forget that our inner excitement may make us appear foolish or overdone to the world around us. Nonetheless, to experience the rapture seems justification enough to those captured by its spell.

DASHBOARD PRAYER MEETINGS AND KAMIKAZE EXHIBITIONISM

I remember a brother with whom I used to pray while I was a seminarian. So often we would go to the seminary parking lot and pray together. I soon found a strange addiction to these dashboard prayer meetings. I could see that my friend found such exuberance in them that he often seemed caught up in a kind of spiritual rapport that bound him to a silent enjoyment of God.

Of course, rapture can become a kind of spectacle in which the worshipper sacrifices real worship for an excessive and showy intentionalism.

Pop Christian culture reeks with many of these apparent

excesses. Christian magazines and television resound with this kind of exuberance—and those who haven't yet come to faith, often smile quaintly upon us. Both evangelicals and Catholics seem saccharine or gooey in their devotion. Fish symbols, Chi-Rhos, and those sweet, little Christian breath mints called *New Testamints* call the seriousness of Christian pop-culture into scrutiny. Cultic art prints and statuettes also come to play their part in labeling the faithful as "overboard for Jesus."

But the faithful themselves do not necessarily see themselves as naïve (although the truly naïve rarely suspect their state). They see themselves as devoted and living out their lives lost in the worship of the God who has done so much for them. Nonetheless, the exuberant naïve seem beyond understanding to people who happen to walk in on their worship service or volatile concerts.

This same kind of public disregard seems to have characterized the Corinthian church. These ardent disciples worshipped with a kind of kamikaze exhibitionism that Paul thought took their rapture to a foolhardy stage. Paul does not negate the importance of religious rapture; he merely encourages them to enjoy God and worship more quietly. The apostle simply asked them to install a control switch on their exuberance. The lack of this control had resulted in a frenzy of *glossolalia* and wild praise (1 Cor. 14:22–32).

Where these same phenomena still occur, we need to make sure our excesses do not blunt our reputation for sincerity. We are to worship Christ in spirit, but never make a god of our feelings about God. If our rapture runs amok, it injures our witness. Our exuberance may shut down the wider possibilities of God, who loves all people, even those who misunderstand our wild state of heart.

In some ways it is like a young couple caught up in the throes of first romance. When their rapture tends toward the freest state, they can become almost exhibitionist in their love for each other. Who would begrudge them their loss of propriety? Certainly not those who may have been married so long that they have become dull, exhibiting little evidence either of pride or fire in romance.

Rapture is a perfectly natural—or supernatural—state of being. All the saints have known it. No healthy believer has not felt mystified by the glory of God seen close at hand. Further, those who have experienced it find themselves lost in the need to experience it again. If we never experience it, we can become a people addicted to the blandness of church dogma and the administrivia of haggling committees and moral rule-keeping.

Still, spiritual rapture is an advanced state of being filled with the Holy Spirit. To enjoy the rapture he imparts is, to some degree, exotic. And this wonderful state goes beyond merely living out our lives as a drab function of our monotone Bible studies and drowsy sermons. We feel we've got it made with God because we've memorized rules and regulations. If only we just wear our Christian T-shirts, tune our radios to Christian music and do Bible study one night a week, we think we are a real witness to those around us.[2]

In rapture we become a people who are more than people. We transcend those biological and anthropological sciences that name us *homo sapiens*. We become far more than *homo sapiens*; we are *homo mysterius*, otherworldly creatures characterized by the joy of being filled with God's addictive love.

How then shall we define this word rapture? I know of no better way than to see it as a kind of "highly effusive love." When we use the word in a secular sense, it always has to do with the sort of delirious love experienced in human intimacy. When a couple enjoy each other in sexual union, the word rapture becomes most appropriate. It is as if they are transported from the present to somewhere more glorious. Rapture of any sort has about it an element of transport. It is as moving as it is resplendent, but its resplendence cannot be defined.

No dictionary can make this real to us; it is too experiential to be defined. Things real but indefinable we call mystery, and mystery lies at the heart of rapture. Those who have known it attest to its reality by their failure to define it. Dumb before its power, they confess, "The greatest meaning that may be known is buried in a mystery so deep that I cannot express its reality to fit within the mind of another." Still, it is a state to be praised, for its sweetness lingers in the heart and leaves all those who have experienced it with the need to experience it again and again.

Certainly this is true when we are filled with the effervescent love of God. Just as those who have known it cannot define it, those under its captivity may allow their exuberance to get out of hand. At such a moment—at the peak of rapture— we not only are at a loss to define it, we also can no longer explain it to those who witness our captivity to its spell. We know only that to be lost in the joy of knowing God is, in itself, a kind of elation. If we are spiritually healthy we never get addicted to the elation, but to the Savior. And we find rapture an immense aid in carrying us over the rough and painful places of our lives.

I once visited a cave in Spain where Saint Teresa of Avila and Saint John of the Cross became so lost in the rapture of their prayers, that they levitated—at least, this is what the natives say. Whether they actually levitated may be questioned, but surely they experienced a buoyancy in their joy. dc Talk speaks of this buoyancy in *Jesus Freaks*. Many modern martyrs have suffered much for Jesus. Still, their suffering was somewhat assuaged by the joy they felt when praising the Lord in their moments of extreme witness. They allow their rapture to make of them contemporary revolutionaries. Many of these contemporary revolutionaries cannot read or write, but they do openly share the Good News. One man in Bangladesh spoke about a Muslim attack on his home: "They burned my house. But they cannot burn Jesus from our hearts." Another Bangladeshi Christian rides his bicycle through villages, even though they threaten to cut off his feet.[3] Clearly this disciple offers his testimony to be borne on the wings of his own inner transport.

But it is not only our contemporaries who have experienced this wonderful feeling of elation. It has been a constant joy throughout the church. Tertullian asked in the second century, "Has truth ever been discovered without God? . . . By whom has Christ ever been explored without the Holy Spirit? Has the Holy Spirit ever been attained without the mysterious gift of faith?"[4] Tertullian himself said it was the Holy Spirit who often overwhelmed us with this wonderful feeling of joyous elation, perhaps even to the point of madness.

One thing that always accompanies joy is the feeling that, whatever happens, a kind of absurd happiness overarches all of the woes that we Christians may endure. I believe this is true of the martyrs, right up to the chopping block. They always realized that whatever Jesus required of them, all of it would be compensated by their extreme love for him—by their rapture. G.K. Chesterton wrote: "Jesus promised his disciples three things—that they would be completely fearless, absurdly happy, and in constant trouble."[5]

As we examine our case for walking with Jesus Christ, let us go on to understand that the Holy Spirit supplies this marvelous joy that makes possible our negotiation of the rough passages of life. We could not negotiate all the rough places of life were we not in love with a God who, through his Holy Spirit, buries us from time to time in the great reality of rapture. For rapture, definable or not, is the wall of reality on which hangs the elusive trappings of heightened religious experience.

RAPTURE AS ENERGY

Rapture supplies us with a kind of energy for our life in Christ. When we begin to tap this energy, the Holy Spirit gives us triumph over the more debilitating circumstances of our lives. Then we begin to see power hidden within our rapture. So we gain an inner energy, through the Holy Spirit, over whatever God asks us to endure, be it death itself.

The Jesuits who in 1597 began to bring Christian missions to Japan often faced unheard of pain. Much of this pain is recorded in the marvelous novel *Silence* by Shusaku Endo. Some of those missionaries faced death by crucifixion. But before they were crucified, many of their Samurai tormentors had already mutilated, tortured, and maimed them. Gonzolo Garcia was among those fearless martyrs who faced both amputation and death.

> When Gonzolo Garcia arrived, he stepped forward to greet Francis Rodriguez Pinto, one of the two Jesuits there to minister to the prisoners. "My good friend, God be with you. I am going to heaven today. Please give a hearty hug

to Friar Gonzalez on my behalf next time you see him."
Then Brother Garcia turned to the cross nearest him. "Is
this one mine?" he asked a soldier. It was not. So the soldier
led him to another a short distance away. When he arrived
there, he knelt and embraced it.[6]

It is amazing how his elated soul, with rapturous resolve,
faced his cross with more cheer than might be imagined. It
must have baffled his killers.

Whatever we are asked to endure, rapture and the sense
of excitement that sometimes accompanies it make it possible
for us to serve the fullest agenda of God. Such challenges lead
us to come face-to-face with Acts 5:29, where the apostles
make it clear to the officials of Judaism that they would not
cease to preach the gospel. They would go on preaching even
if it meant their death: We don't obey people, we obey God.
This kind of forceful testimony, I believe, can be given only by
those who have accepted this innate joy as a kind of energy
and power.

The martyrs we most remember never seemed morose as
they went to their death. Often they sang hymns, quoted brave
scriptures or made positive statements of encouragement to
those next in line to die. Where did they receive this energy?
The most obvious answer is that their energy came from their
spiritual rapture.

Richard Wurmbrand, a marvelous saint in our own day,
spent fourteen years in a Communist prison cell in Romania.
He wrote of all the joy he found in facing his harsh trials. The
Holy Spirit of God supplied him with a kind of rapture. "In our
darkest hours of torture, the Son of man came to us, making
the prison walls shine like diamonds and filling the cell with

light. We would not have given up this joy for that of kingly palaces."[7] Always and ever an energy comes to us so that we may endure all that our obedience to God might require of us. In Acts 1:8, Jesus says to the disciples, "Ye shall receive power after the Holy Ghost is come upon you"(KJV). In the Spirit's power lies the exuberance of our resolve.

I suspect it is little different than a football team that loses every game at the start of the season, but which suddenly finds itself caught up in a winning streak. Before long, the joy of winning supplies these athletes with the energy to continue their winning streak. Often they feel caught up in a kind of joy that makes them unbeatable.

A recent film called *The Rookie* focuses upon a man who in midlife comes to understand that he has never achieved his great dream of pitching in the major leagues. Bit by bit, his friends encourage him to leave his fear behind in order to advance to the "Big Show" despite his age. Off he goes to soar into prominence as a great pitcher. What made the difference? He gets caught up with a kind of enthusiastic energy that supplies him with the power to achieve the dreams he thought he had left behind.

In a similar but more serious sense, rapture supplies immense energy for living the Christian life, though in less dramatic ways than the martyrs demonstrated. Men and women with ordinary resolve reach out to take advantage of this vitality.

RAPTURE AS MYSTERY

Mystery is a kind of love affair inexplicable in human terms. It is indeed elusive.

For the last twenty years of my life I have been caught up

in reading the tales of the saints. I do repent that for many of my years as an evangelical, these heroes of the historical church remained inaccessible to me. But once I discovered them, I found myself poking around more liturgical bookstalls and even a great many Catholic bookstores. The ordinary evangelical presses held less for me sometimes than traditional bookstores, and I read ever further into Paulist Press publications. I felt hungry for a new kind of reading that supplied to me the centuries-old stories of the heroes of God's saving mystery.

Now and then I caught glimpses of these heroes in the secular arts. The Broadway play *Agnes of God* tells the story of a beautiful woman in love with God. Her love of God causes her to remain oblivious to all the causes and happenings around her. She is in love with the mystery of godliness.

One can understand why Saint Paul puts so much emphasis on this mystery of godliness. We find a deliciousness in faith when we learn that we cannot give the reasons that we exist or explain the power of faith in our lives. We are powerless to explain our fondest identity in Christ to those around us, because all that God is doing through our lives is indeed mysterious.

Tertullian said a long time ago that our Lord Jesus Christ named himself "truth" and not "custom." How true that is, yet how quickly churches get caught up in things customary. Worship planning can become perfunctory, if not at least customary. Worship for many seems something dull to be done, rather than a fearsome plunge into mystery. To think ourselves creative in worship has become customary. One gets the feeling that worship is a highly competitive disease between suburban churches. It is not so much that they worship God, but that they worship their own creativity. In fact, they worship their worship.

A plethora of books claim to explain how to become creative. Unfortunately, the mystery of Godliness is not to be found in books on how to get creative. Nor would the energy that comes from rapture ever become a mere addendum to the work of worship committees. No! It comes from a person hungry for union with Christ, a person whose very character gets caught up in the joy of walking with the Lord and being filled with his presence. It is for this reason that Jim Elliot wrote: "God, I pray Thee, light these idle sticks of my life, that I may burn for thee. Consume my life, my God, for it is Thine."[8]

Rapture befits the eager heart. What then does this mystery actually mean? It means this: mystery drives the person of God. To have tasted this elixir is to know that we don't know everything. We relish in our ignorance the reality of wonderful things we could never define.

Unfortunately, the word mystery has lost its force in this bright, new millennium. Why? Malcom Muggeridge says we lost the mystery because the Western culture made imprudent trades. We decided that we didn't need the mystery of godliness and so we amplified the mystery of sexuality. Muggeridge believed that in the closing years of the twentieth century, sexuality provided the only mysticism to be found among secular souls. People had traded their need to know God for something somewhat mysterious but less ethereal.

Spirituality and sexuality do seem to approximate each other. There can be no question that these two primary forces operate in the lives of all human beings: the need for God and the more instant, fiery need for something temporarily satisfying. When spiritual mystery reaches its height, however, it is by far the more beautiful and potent of the two forces. It is vastly more transcendent. Further, it operates out of all place and time. It captivates us, not for a few brief minutes at a time, but for vast decades of our lives and careers, our fortunes and our world view. No wonder that Clement of Alexandria wrote, "Martyrdom is fullness, not because it finishes a human life, but because it brings love to the fullest point."[9] Clement makes it very clear that ultimate rapture brings us directly to the gates of heaven.

It is interesting that those who end their lives, and consequently their earthly walk with God, often describe it in terms of rapture. The saints, I suppose, never felt more rapture than when they stood at the gates of heaven.

It is easy to see that when you walk with Jesus Christ and hunger after his reality, the natural thing to talk about as death approaches is that exotic and ecstatic union with Christ. And this final exuberance is nothing more than the enhancement of that which we have craved all of our lives. For this reason Fructuosus wrote of impending martyrdom:

> Believe me! What you see happening before your eyes is no
> punishment; it will be over quickly, and doesn't take away
> life, but gives it. O happy souls who pass through this tem-
> porary fire to ascend into heaven to God.[10]

This then becomes the height of mystery, a mystery that heightens our joy and makes possible a glad traversing across the rough areas of our lives. This great mystery envelops us and, like a giant limousine, sweeps us between worlds.

RAPTURE AS TRANSFORMATION

The wind comes and goes as it pleases, "So is everyone who is born of the Spirit," said Jesus (John 3:8, NKJV). The wind is not just Jesus' idea of mystery. There is a kind of sweep and power in the idea of the word. We looked at this symbol earlier in the book and have no need to develop it further now, except to say that implicit in the idea of wind is rapture.

When the Holy Spirit comes on the Day of Pentecost in Acts 2, one cannot help but notice two things. First, he comes in wind and fire; and second, he changes the mood of the day to rapture. As the wind blows, this rapture begins to transform these ordinarily quiet, Aramaic-speaking people—who perhaps know little of this world's great intellectual truth—into fearless warriors against the spiritual status quo. These happy and bold new converts tumble into the streets in the sheer mood of joy, an ecstatic mood that captures the entire book of Acts. It moves in power from martyr to martyr and convert to convert.

But the book of Acts does not stand alone in getting caught up in rapture as transformation. Rapture sweeps down across history, claiming fields of martyrs, establishing thousands upon thousands of churches, spreading the Kingdom of God like wildfire across Europe, England, America, and now the third and fourth worlds.

This transformation begins when we see rapture as a viable force for change within our own lives. We must, however, give the Spirit room to do all that he will do. We must make a place for the kind of rapture he inspires within our churches—yet too often we turn from this. Why? We fear rapture because rapture makes us afraid that spiritual things may get out of hand.

For years, those evangelicals who don't speak in tongues have feared the tongues movement. They fear that it would sweep into a congregation and destroy all the previous propriety that had identified the congregation as "normal." But real change can never occur until we lay aside this fear and give a hearty welcome to the idea of rapture as an important kind of talk. It seems to me that the Holy Spirit is a Spirit of love who moves against all human conditions for propriety and makes us uncomfortable with the edgy contingencies of our faith. This does not mean we have to talk in tongues to know rapture. Rapture may never be defined so one-dimensionally. But just as ardor will have a way out at a football game, so we cannot talk about the greatness of God in deadpan liturgy. The Spirit always shoves and pushes and elbows his way into our midst with great joy. Archbishop Michael Ramsey of the Church of England wrote, "We must avoid binding the Spirit by our stupidity and our narrowness and lack of faith."[11] This is why we must give the Spirit room in our lives. I believe we need to invite the Spirit to move in power within us.

And how shall we speak of this uncomfortable joy he brings? We shall speak of this joy as it is in its fullness. It is the joy of transformation. Paul says in 2 Corinthians 5:17 that if any person be in Christ, he is a new creature, completely transformed, changed from something earthbound and dogged with heavy leaden boots into something with wings that fly. In the opinion I long ago stated in an epigram of a little book called *Guardians of the Singreale*:

Earth holds a strange power that binds men to its crust
so that ponderous men are bound in the dust

but the wind whispers tales of a force in the sky
and those with the courage to scorn dust can fly.[12]

KNOWN BY JOY

God calls us to become a people known by our joy. He calls us
to become a people who understand that rapture is a legitimate
mood. We are called to live out what one of the martyrs said so
long ago: "Joy is the most infallible proof of the presence of
God."

And if the presence of God be equated to the Holy Spirit,
as I believe it must, then joy is indeed the most infallible proof
of the Holy Spirit's presence among us.

UNION WITH CHRIST

The life, the self-sacrifice, the blood, which they are ready to shed for their faith, is the greatest argument for Christianity presented by the underground church. It forms what the renowned missionary in Africa, Albert Schweitzer, called "the sacred fellowship of Those who have the mark of pain," The fellowship to which Jesus, the Man of sorrows, belonged. The underground church is united by a bond of love toward its Savior. The same bond unites the members of the church with each other. Nobody in the world can defeat them.[1]

RICHARD WURMBRAND

At the center of all real faith lies a hunger that exceeds dogma. Dorothy Sayers said long ago that in Christianity, the doctrine was the dance. She meant to emphasize, of course, that the teaching content of our faith is the faith. The statement is true, but must not be allowed to abrogate the importance of the feeling side of faith.

At the center of all vital faith lies a hunger, the hunger to know and experience a closeness with Christ. It is for this reason that we who love him often feel it important to talk about Jesus as our personal Savior. Who would want a distant and impersonal one?

All saints in all ages, whether in the Old or New Testament, have expressed the need to feel a close sense of the presence of the Spirit of God. David cries out in the fifty-first Psalm, "Cast me not away from thy presence and take not thy holy spirit from me" (Psalm 51:11, KJV). It was David's great passion to live in oneness with the Spirit of God. His heart cry of agony in Psalm 51 expresses a deep longing to have this closeness restored, which he damaged through his affair with Bathsheba. David learned what all God lovers know, that sin is a roadblock to a close relationship with God.

THE MARK OF ALL GOD-LOVERS

Union with Christ is a three-word attempt to define that great hunger that marks the souls of all those who love God. Exactly what is this hunger? It drives us from the inside out. Again, the Psalmist says, "As the deer pants for the water brooks, so pants my soul for You, O God" (Ps. 42:1, NKJV).

It is increasingly hard to find churches led by men and women who truly hunger after God. We have traded in our hunger for God for "churchy" clubs, leagues and societies.

We've gotten better at gymnasiums than we are sanctuaries. In many churches it seems easier to learn to golf than to learn to pray. The church in many cases has become a little vaccination of boredom that keeps us from getting a real case of Spirit hunger.

In a telltale anecdote, an alien visits earth, where he attends three different churches. One was Wesleyan, the second Baptist, and the third Presbyterian. Reporting back to his overlords, he said, "When I visited the Wesleyans, all I heard was, 'Fire! Fire!' When I visited the Baptists, all I heard was, 'Water! Water!' In the Presbyterian church, all I heard was, 'Order! Order!'"[2]

This humorous little anecdote expresses the empty forms that often lie at the heart of denominational groups. It is not that these particular denominational emphases are wrong; it's that they can become a substitute for developing a membership that focuses on Jesus alone. Those of us who live and serve in these denominations should clamor for the kind of hunger that characterized the saints.

After reading a great many books on the Holy Spirit, I can testify that most have been written by academicians interested in informing us on who the Holy Spirit is, or how he acts in the devoted life, or the nature of his place in church history. Only occasionally did I run across a book on the Holy Spirit where the author takes a big step toward identifying with the hungering saints of the ages. Yet only these men and women write out of that deep thirst for God, the thirst of a deer panting after a water brook.

Further, it seems to me that those authors with less interest in obtaining a formal education were more likely to show an interest in pursuing a real experience with the Holy Spirit.

Doctor E.F. Scott long ago wrote of the importance of the relationship of the Holy Spirit to the Christian's experience: "It has been strongest in times of religious awakening, when men have grown suddenly aware that the truths they clung to half-mechanically are the great realities . . . They have felt themselves possessed with a quickening and uplifting power, which seemed to come directly out of a higher world."[3] It is this experiential hunger that has driven me all my life to know and understand the lives of the saints. The saints have captured a place in history, not because they had a desire to inform us about God, but because they had a driving hunger to experience God as much as God may be experienced in this present life.

If the Bible were only a book of information about God, we should all too soon tire of it. It was designed, rather, to entreat us to move into the depths of God and to experience his fullness, a fullness expressed in those three little words, *Union with Christ*.

UNION WITH CHRIST

It is a wonderful thing to understand that no union, no friendship, no relationship is quite so vital to us as union with Christ. Why not? Because all other relationships get blocked by at least three things:

> Surface relationships do not nourish us in any eternal way;
> Most human relationships are transient and fleeting;
> The nearness of mere human relationships sometimes blocks our desire to pursue a less convenient union with the Father;

Regarding this last point, Saint John of the Cross said that we should pray not to have more friends, but to have enemies. For so long as we have one other earthly friend, he taught, we will seek the counsel of that friend rather than to retreat to the wiser counsel of the Father. And thus, those we depend upon in this life sometimes unwittingly keep us from going to the best source of information.

Union with Christ triumphs over all other friendships. The Holy Spirit compels us to hunger for union with Christ. Union with Christ is driven by that same hope of crossing the thresholds that often exist between mere earthly friends. And why is this so? Because no matter how close we would like to draw to anyone else, there exists between even the closest of friends a kind of "personality threshold" that bars the entrance into the inner sanctum of their inner selves. Closeness is possible, but not utter union.

This same threshold operates between ourselves and the Holy Spirit. Even when our relationship with the Spirit becomes very real, it remains so inward that we find our longing for union somewhat thwarted. Still, in select moments of our lives, we do indeed see across that vast abyss to the place where Jesus dwells. Then a kind of glory descends upon us and we feel that we have pulled these two reaching worlds together and that Christ's Holy Spirit really does reside within our hearts.

At this moment of reality, our union with Christ becomes so intense that we begin to understand that this is all that matters. We feel as though we are inseparable—or at least we desire it so—from this union. Because of the Holy Spirit, we feel it is possible to become one with Jesus Christ.

Jesus prayed in the Gospel of John that we would be one

with him, even as he is one with the Father. This sense of union that he prayed for and desired for his followers, inhabits the soul and becomes a restless longing in the hearts of those who seek him. Augustine said, "Our hearts are restless, O Lord, until they find their rest in Thee." Augustine, I believe, was speaking of that intense hunger resolved only when we achieve (or believe we have achieved or are close to achieving) the wonderful state of union with Christ. And why is this union so dear? Because it speaks to us from the inside out and tells us exactly where we stand with our Father at all times.

In A.D. 851 after the Moors invaded Spain, two women known as Nunia and Alodia stood condemned to death for their faith. Before their execution they endured countless threats of torture and pain and harassment. This fear of torture drove these sisters in a strong way to speak of the true values of life. Their final testimony speaks almost entirely of the Holy Spirit fostering union with Christ. "O judge!" they cried, "How is it that you command us to turn away from true godliness, since God has made it known to us that no one is a richer or a better bridegroom than Jesus Christ, our Savior?"[4]

Nunia and Alodia saw, as did most of the martyrs, that union with Christ brought them ever closer to the goal of their redemption: divine oneness inspired by the indwelling Spirit. They believed that union with Christ is the one great Christian value that begins in this world and continues on into the next.

Paul wrote of this same notion in Philippians 1:21–24:

> For to me, to live is Christ, and to die is gain. But if I live on in the flesh, this will mean fruit from my labor; yet what I shall choose I cannot tell. For I am hard-pressed between the two, having a desire to depart and be with Christ, which

is far better. Nevertheless to remain in the flesh is more needful for you. (NKJV)

One can see in Paul's longing his preference for death over life. This desire heightens every part of our being and feeds our hunger for complete union with Christ.

THE AGENT OF UNION WITH CHRIST

As we hunger for union with Christ, we begin to understand that the Spirit makes it possible. He is, as we have said throughout this book, the near side of the Trinity.

One sees evidences of the Spirit in both testaments, Old and New. So let us take a look at those scriptures that appear in the Old Testament. Many times the saints of the Old Testament talked simply about how the Holy Spirit came to them and took possession of them, where he is generally called the Spirit of the LORD. Observe his prominence in these pre-New Testament heroes of the faith:

The Spirit of the LORD took possession of Gideon
(Judges 6:34).
The woman bore a son, and called his name Samson.
. . . and the Spirit of the LORD began to stir him . . . And
the Spirit of the LORD came mightily upon him
(Judges 13:24–25; 14:6).
The Spirit of the LORD came mightily upon him (Saul).
. . . The Spirit of the LORD departed from Saul
(1 Samuel 10:10; 16:14).
These are the last words of David . . . "The Spirit of the
LORD speaks by me"
(2 Samuel 23:1–2).

And Elisha said (to Elijah), "I pray you, let me
inherit a double share of your spirit"
(2 Kings 2:9).

In the New Testament we call the Spirit of the Lord, the
Holy Spirit. He becomes our source, our agent of union with
God. But what happens to us when life becomes hard and we
fight for meaning and hope *in extremis?* What are we to do
when life requires more of us and we seem to have too little of
this thing that we call union with Christ? Léon Joseph Cardinal Suenens gives us a clue as to the importance of God's involvement with us at the hour of our greatest need. He makes
it clear that faith teaches us all we need to know. Suenens here
quotes from the French priest, Caffarel, and teaches us again
that the Holy Spirit gives us the promise of his indwelling support through any moment of crisis. Father Caffarel says: "The
hour of suffering is the hour of God . . . We must admit that
we are lost, surrender ourselves as lost and praise the Lord who
saves us."[5] Always the hour of suffering causes us to rely most
on the inward presence of Christ. The presence of suffering or
duress or pain also causes us to treasure our sense of union with
Christ.

But what are we talking about when we speak about this
union with Christ? Cardinal Suenens warns us: Jesus did not
present aridity as the normal condition of the Christian life.[6]
Saint John of the Cross and Saint Teresa of Avila desired union
with Christ so they might find a way of devising a customary
Christian walk that would supply them with the confidence of
the Holy Spirit and his continuing presence even in moments of
pain, hunger, or need. They wanted this union not in life's needy
times alone, but also in the full and better moments of life.

How does this indwelling Christ work in his fullness? "Sometimes, the Holy Spirit draws a man so completely to Himself that he forgets all created things and gives himself entirely to contemplation of God . . . In thus praying, the soul may again forget the world and repose in God alone, only to return once more to her prayer for all mankind."[7] The Spirit is not only the agent of how God fills our lives; he is the basis of our union with Christ, wherever our journey takes us. This union depends upon our living with the indwelling Spirit, who will always live on the inside of us. This is the heart of union with Christ.

> Once he is inside, everything is different for the traveler. The bright flames on the hearth leap up to greet him, the heat begins to envelop, to penetrate him, his face lights up in the glow, he reaches out his two hands, and his numb limbs begin to lose their numbness. A sort of osmosis begins; the brightness of the flames penetrates his very being . . . We are not alone any more, we know we are guided by the Holy Spirit; our life unfolds in response to him . . . we dispossess ourselves, our being is possessed by God. The void is filled . . . Their life, nourished by the fire of the Holy Spirit, becomes fire in its turn. Is not this the fire of which Jesus spoke when he said: "I have come to bring fire to the earth . . ."(Luke 12:49)?[8]

Once he is inside of us, we become travelers indeed.

The Spirit is the agent of this union with God, who is our guide to the pilgrimage of life. Christians have often thought of life as a pilgrimage and themselves as travelers, reading the road map to union. But if we envision ourselves as travelers filled with the Holy Spirit, it ought to occur to us (and does, I hope), that we travel with him—and his roadmap to union—always deep inside us.

But how are we to define this pilgrimage? In the Middle Ages there were two kinds of pilgrimages. One is the type described by Chaucer in *Canterbury Tales*, where pilgrims flocked to a particular shrine at a particular place. At this shrine visitors held prayer vigils and made offerings.

The Celts and the Irish had a much different definition of pilgrimage. They fostered saints like Brendan and Godric, who saw themselves on a lifelong pilgrimage. The only shrine they sought would come when they crossed the grave to "the other side." In the meantime, they carried their shrine with them in the altar of their hearts: the shrine of the Holy Spirit, the wrist-locks of union with Christ. No pilgrim or pilgrimage of this type ever was alone, for the indwelling Spirit who lived inside them made the journey with them.

MERGER

We all desire this hunger for union. Augustine said, "Not your gifts, Lord, but you!"[9]

The ultimate hunger for union is cast in the concept of merger. Augustine didn't want the things of this world that God might supply him. Neither did he long for the mere spiritual blessings God might supply him. Augustine wanted God himself. This, I believe, is the last step of maturity in our walk of faith.

Too often we intercede in prayer only to beg stuff from God's good storehouse. "Lord, won't you please give me a Mercedes-Benz?" lies at the other pole of our maturity. As long as intercession begs God for stuff, we remain infantile in our walk with God. When we are full grown we will beg God for himself. So it is with every mature believer: none who hunger for the good stuff of God's abundance, will fail to satisfy their hungry souls. Those desperate for God want only God himself.

Earlier we discussed our fear of the Holy Spirit's intrusion into our lives. Later we discussed the fear of not yielding to the Spirit. But at the heart of this great paradox we find those who hunger for union with Christ. These desire the presence of the Holy Spirit, the ever-intrusive God. These know that they must have God intruding into their affairs or their affairs are of no consequence.

All the saints, however, lived with the constant danger that to submit oneself completely to God and to care only about his invasion and union with Christ might leave the church without an adequate sense of ministry. This distortion in seeking God can lead at last to a contemplative life characterized by a sterile ministry.

ONE-NESS EQUALS SELF-CRUCIFIXION

Four steps lead to complete union with Christ.

1. The decentralizing of the ego.

In this step, the person seeking union with Christ comes to realize that self must be cleared out of the way to make room for the approach of Jesus Christ. Jesus said this himself in Luke 9:23: "If anyone would come after me, he must deny himself and take up his cross daily and follow me" (NIV). There is a real sense in which the ego must be decentralized. There must come a time when the big "I" steps out of the way for the big

"Him." When we take this step of trading the "Him" for the "I," we have learned the secret of decentralizing the ego.

Yet how is this to be done practically? While each of us bears a strong love of self (and we honor that self, often to a fault), we also try to make sure that the self never gets in the way of God. We labor all our lives between opposite poles. On the one hand, we lean toward Galatians 2:20, where Paul says, "I am crucified with Christ, nevertheless I live." Paul is doing what every great believer has tried to do: get self out of the way so that Christ might become all in all. On the other hand, we also drift toward that simple little rhyme we learned as children: "I love myself, I love myself, I pick me up and hug myself. I put my arm around my waist and got so fresh I slapped my face." It is very difficult to move away from this inner self that we adore. We spend our lives protecting it, enhancing it, decorating it, dressing it, and pushing it outward toward great modes of career and achievement. Naturally, this self that has been so much the center of our life-long attention, dies very hard. It is hard to decentralize the ego—but this must be done or we can never make room for step two.

2. Making a conscious throne in the center of our lives.

It is difficult to move to the center of our lives, where we take self from the throne and put Jesus there instead. Yet no disciple has ever begun the process of union with Christ without first making this conscious step—setting up a conscious throne in the center of the heart and life.

I mentioned in a previous book about being on the Oral Roberts Campus when Oral Roberts had his vision of a nine hundred foot Jesus. I felt conflicted about this gargantuan vision, because it seemed to me that most people suffered from having no vision of Jesus at all. That day as I spoke in chapel, I told the audience, "I invite you not to this gargantuan Christ which stands a thousand feet tall. Rather, I invite you to turn inward to the throne of your heart where a little thumbnail size Christ occupies a thumbnail sized throne. It is to the inward arena of this God-conscious throne that I invite you to come and submit to Jesus."

All union with Christ must somewhere decentralize the ego and then create a conscious throne where we may period-ically retreat to receive our instruction and orders for all that makes us one with Christ.

3. Losing the ambition of the ego.

All egos, to a certain degree, need to plan for the future, lest they live a pointless and haphazard life. So once again our heav-enly Father asks us to live with tension. We are foolish if we plan no course for our lives. As the cliché has it, to fail to plan is to plan to fail. We are foolish if we take no steps to direct our future. But we are equally foolish if we let our own plans and ambitions drive us into workaholism or even alcoholism. Cor-porate achievement, for instance, is not the only aspect of greatness. The question is, why do we want to achieve, and what drives our motivation to get on in the world in the first place?

By slaying the ambitions of our ego we deal with these sorts of things. A forty-thousand-a-year factory employee might be tempted to look to Bill Gates with some longing. Or perhaps the thirty-thousand-a-year mechanic might look to the recent state lottery winner with a jaundiced eye. But the real question is not how much you have, but why do you want it in the first place? What possible good does it do in the long run of eternity? These kinds of questions occupy those who truly pursue union with Christ. They have decided to make self-crucifixion the very essence of their relationship with Christ. Only such self-denial can give them the kind of union where Jesus supplants their petty dreams with spiritual greatness.

4. A desire for "merger."

This is the most mysterious and mystical of all the steps just described, for in fact, it is indescribable. Those who have experienced union with Christ often experience it only after they have come out of some "dark night of the soul," as Saint John of the Cross put it. This union with Christ comes when they have reached the end of themselves and when their despair is about to break forth into light. These states do not come frequently in our lives; they come as need and life circumstance mandate.

How shall we understand this step? I like to compare it to the experience of astronauts who come back to us after orbiting the earth or the moon. They have lived out their scientific ventures in a wasteland of daunting temperatures and an oxygenless emptiness.

At times in our own lives with Christ we, too, are spiritually in space. Bleak, dull, and fruitless seem our lives. The world around us looks barren and empty. We, too, are removed from our soul's best home. But in achieving union with Christ, we become like those cosmic sailors. As these bold venturers re-enter earth's atmosphere, they come through a time of high stress. The heat and friction of reentering the atmosphere engulfs them in flame, a fiery baptismal reentry to the quiet and beauty of the earth. Their vehicle becomes literally a sphere of flame. For one brief moment or two, the intense heat shuts off all communication with earth. Then comes the breakthrough and the greens and blues and the pleasantness of the planet they left for their long, sterile adventure in barren space, become real to them once again.

In such a way I see union with Christ. Sometimes in our despair we find it impossible to define ourselves spiritually or to reach any real levels of God-communication. Then, all of a sudden, we find ourselves in this wonderful pattern of breakthrough into the very presence of Jesus Christ. At such moments this presence becomes so real that we tremble with joy. Great fear and great elation come at once, an elixir so delicious that it can lead only to the hunger to experience it again.

But union with Christ must not be restricted to those very special moments when we enjoy a heightened awareness of God, possessing, controlling, and owning us. The best concept of union with Christ is a conscious, daily walk, fueled by the disciplines of prayer and Bible study. This leads us to a moment-by-moment dependency with that thumbnail sized Christ who rules from life's center, through every moment of elation or despair, glory or business as usual. Only such a constant view of union with Christ can carry us at last across the threshold of the here and now into the presence of Jesus Christ, forever.

OUR EARNEST REDEMPTIVE SEAL

Union with Christ must be stated in terms of all that is most valuable in our lives. Yet we must never forget that the Spirit of God makes possible our union. It is he who comes to us, who indwells us and who is our inner seal and guarantee that we indeed are possessed with Christ.

The Holy Spirit is our earnest, redemptive seal. He provides the irrefutable evidence that we indeed are a people owned by the powerful Savior, who once left the glories of heaven and agreed to live in such mortal hovels as human beings.

STILL HUNGRY

The meal we promised in the preface is done. You're still hungry, aren't you? Me, too!

But do not despise me for putting so little on your plate. Life is defined not by what we eat, but what we hunger for. There will be other tables, other meals, and each of them will offer you some kind of nourishment. Still, the Spirit of God will bless your hunger, for each time you pause to enjoy his reality, you will commune—become one with him—and this oneness will become the only appetite of your life that ever mattered.

NOTES

❧

PREFACE

[1] Léon Joseph Cardinal Suenens, *A New Pentecost?* (NY: The Seabury Press, 1975), xiii.

INTRODUCTION: AT THE LEFT HAND OF GOD

[1] Schaff/Wace translation; http://www.angelfire.com/ny4/djw/epiphanius.creed.html.

[2] Dr. H. Wheeler Robinson, as quoted by Henry P. Van Dusen in *Spirit, Son and Father* (NY: Charles Scribner's Sons, 1958), 9.

[3] R.C. Sproul, *The Mystery of the Holy Spirit* (Wheaton, IL: Tyndale House Publishers, Inc., 1990), 76.

[4] Thomas C. Oden, *Life in the Spirit* (San Francisco: HarperCollins Publishers, 1992), 6-7.

[5] Agnes Ozment, as quoted by Yves M.J. Congar in *The Word and the Spirit* (San Francisco: Harper & Row Publishers, 1984), 51.

CHAPTER 1: THE WIND

[1] Calvin Miller, *The Song, from The Singer Trilogy* (Downers Grove, IL: InterVarsity Press, 1977), 189-190.

[2] George Barna, *What American's Believe* (CA: Regal Books, 1991)

[3] *A Primer for Preachers* (Grand Rapids, Mich.: Baker Book House, 1999).

CHAPTER 2: THE FIRE

[1] Hildegard of Bingen, *Symphonia,* p. 143, as quoted by Oden in *Life in the Spirit,* 43.

[2] Mary Skobtsova, as quoted by dc Talk in *Jesus Freaks Vol II* (Minneapolis, MN: Bethany House Publishing, 2002), 109.

[3] Charles Finney, as quoted by Calvin Miller in *Spirit, Word and Story* (Nashville, TN: Word Publishing, 1989), 29.

[4] As quoted by Suenens, *A New Pentecost?,* 67.

[5] Chiara Lubich, as quoted by Suenens in *A New Pentecost?,* 67.

CHAPTER 3: THE OIL

[1] Prayer from the Eucharist, as quoted by Suenens in *A New Pentecost?,* 47.

[2] Taken from the *National Bulletin on the Liturgy,* Number 37, (January, 1973), 49, as quoted by Suenens in *A New Pentecost,* 42.

[3] Herbert F. Brokering, as quoted by Sproul in *The Mystery of the Holy Spirit,* 114.

[4] Gerald G. May, *Will and Spirit* (San Francisco: Harper & Row Publishers, 1982), 143-144.

CHAPTER 4: PRESENCE

[1] Thomas Aquinas, as quoted by Oden in *Life in the Spirit,* 211.

[2] Dorothy Sayers, as quoted in Robertson McQuilkin's *Life in the Spirit* (Nashville, TN: Broadman and Holman Publishers, 2000), 100.

[3] As quoted in dc Talk, *Jesus Freaks, Vol II,* 224.

[4] As quoted in Calvin Miller's *Once Upon a Tree* (West Monroe, LA: Howard, 2002), 43.

[5] As quoted in dc Talk, *Jesus Freaks, Vol II,* 135.

[6] McQuilkin, *Life in the Spirit,* 100.

[7] McQuilkin, *Life in the Spirit,* 106-107.

[8] Rachel Scott, as quoted in *Jesus Freaks Vol II,* 58.

CHAPTER 5: TRIUMPH

[1] Martin Luther King, Jr., as quoted by dc Talk in *Jesus Freaks Vol II*, 44.

[2] See W. Ian Thomas, *The Saving Life of Christ* (Grand Rapids: Zondervan, 1989).

[3] McQuilkin, *Life in the Spirit*, 241.

[4] McQuilkin, *Life in the Spirit*, 193.

CHAPTER 6: ILLUMINATION OF THE WORD MADE PRINT

[1] H. Wheeler Robinson, as quoted by Henry P. Van Dusen in *Spirit, Son and Father* (NY: Charles Scribner's Sons, 1958), 33.

[2] Lisa Beamer, *Let's Roll* (Wheaton, IL: Tyndale House, 2002), 220.

[3] Clark Pinnock, *Bibliotheca Sacra*, Oct-Dec, 1967, as quoted in Charles Swindoll, *The Tardy Oxcart* (Nashville: Word, 1998), 49.

[4] As quoted in Charles Swindoll, *The Tardy Oxcart* (Nashville, TN: Word Books, 1998), 46.

[5] As quoted in Swindoll, *The Tardy Oxcart*, 52-53.

[6] As quoted in Swindoll, *The Tardy Oxcart*, 50.

[7] Beamer, *Let's Roll*, 232.

[8] Fred W. Mueser, *Luther the Preacher* (Minneapolis: Augsburg, 1983), 114.

[9] Mueser, *Luther the Preacher*, 35.

CHAPTER 7: AWAKENING AND EVANGELISM

[1] James Buchanan, *The Office and Work of the Holy Spirit* (Carlisle, PA: The Banner of Truth Trust, 1984), 234.

CHAPTER 8: COUNSEL

[1] Yves M.J. Congar, *The Word and the Spirit* (San Francisco: Harper & Row Publishers, 1986), 58.

[2] Brother Lawrence, Donald Attwater, *The Practice of the Presence of God* (Springfield, IL: Templegate Publishers, 1974), 57, 58.

[3] As quoted in Thomas L. Youngblood and Sandra P. Aldrich, *The Bible Encounters* (Grand Rapids, MI: Zondervan, 2002), 21.

[4] As quoted in Youngblood and Sandra P. Aldrich, *The Bible Encounters*, 81.

[5] Dan Crawford and Calvin Miller, *Prayer Walking* (Nashville, TN: AMG Publishers, 2002), 134-135.

[6] Crawford and Miller, *Prayer Walking*, 135.

[7] St. Paul, Minn: Ruminator Books, 1996.

CHAPTER 9: GRIEF

[1] Gerald G. May, *Will and Spirit*, 91.

[2] Dag Hammarskjöld, *Markings* (NY: Alfred A. Knopf, 1966), 205.

[3] Gerald G. May, *Will and Spirit*, 1.

CHAPTER 10: RAPTURE

[1] Pope Paul VI, as quoted by Suenens, *A New Pentecost?*, 89.

[2] dc Talk, *Jesus Freaks, Vol II*, 4.

[3] dc Talk, *Jesus Freaks, Vol II*, 8.

[4] Tertullian, Christian father and apologist, C.A.D. 150-229, as quoted by dc Talk in *Jesus Freaks, Vol II*, 15.

[5] G.K.Chesterton, British Writer and Christian apologist, 1874-1936, as quoted by d.c. Talk in *Jesus Freaks, Vol II*, 26.

[6] dc Talk, *Jesus Freaks, Vol II*, 39.

[7] Richard Wurmbrand, as quoted by d.c. Talk in *Jesus Freaks, Vol II*, 102.

[8] Jim Elliot, as quoted by d.c. Talk in *Jesus Freaks, Vol II*, 126.

[9] Clement of Alexandria, as quoted by d.c. Talk in *Jesus Freaks, Vol II*, 121.

[10] Fructuosus, as quoted by d.c. Talk in *Jesus Freaks, Vol II*, 294.

[11] Archbishop Michael Ramsey, as quoted by Suenens in a *New Pentecost?*, 177.

[12] Calvin Miller, *Guardians of the Singreale* (San Francisco: Harper & Row Publishers, 1982).

CHAPTER 11: UNION WITH CHRIST

[1] Richard Wurmbrand, as quoted by d.c. Talk in *Jesus Freaks Vol II*, 61.

[2] R.C. Sproul, *The Mystery of the Holy Spirit*, 77.

[3] E.F. Scott, *The Spirit in the New Testament* (London: Hodder & Stroughton Ltd., 1950), vi, 13, vi, 19.

[4] Nunia and Alodia, as quoted by d.c. Talk in *Jesus Freaks Vol II*, 211-212.

[5] H. Caffarel, "Il n'en faut pas plus à Dieu" in *La Chambre Haute 2*, pp. 33-34. (*La Chambre Haute* is a bulletin for prayer groups of the French language published by Editions de Feuy Nouveau, Paris.)

[6] Suenens, *A New Pentecost?*, 61.

[7] Staretz Silouan, *The Undistorted Image*, 1866-1938. Ed. By Archimandrite Sofrony (London: 1958), 81.

[8] Suenens, *A New Pentecost?*, 69-70.

[9] Augustine, as quoted by Suenens in *A New Pentecost?*, 82.